Two Steps Back

For
Frank Ridley, Bert Atkinson and George and Sheila Leslie,
who lived through these policies and opposed them

Two Steps Back

Communists and the
wider labour movement, 1939-1945

A study in the relations between
'vanguard' and class

Sam Bornsten and Al Richardson

MERLIN PRESS

© Sam Bornstein & Al Richardson
First published by Socialist Platform Ltd.

Reprinted 2007 by The Merlin Press Ltd. in association with Socialist
Platform Ltd.

Merlin Press Ltd.
96 Monnow Street
Monmouth
NP25 3EQ
Wales

www.merlinpress.co.uk
www.revolutionary-history.co.uk/socplat.htm
www.revolutionary-history.co.uk

ISBN. 978-0-85036-599-3

British Library Cataloguing in Publication Data
is available from the British Library

Printed in Great Britain by
Lightning Source UK, Milton Keynes

Contents

'There is a tide in the affairs of men
Which taken at the flood leads on to fortune;
Omitted, all the voyage of their life
Is bound in shallows and in miseries'.
Julius Caesar, Act IV, scene 3

'That lot — run a revolution? They couldn't run a whelk
stall!'
George Lansbury

Foreword

Anyone attending a trade union branch these days cannot fail to be
struck with the shifting of political allegiances that is going on. Rank
and file Labour supporters are often seen to be to the 'left' of
Communists, and members of sectarian organisations occasionally
to the 'right' of both of them. 'Moderates' take up extremist attitudes
when disappointed in the scramble for office, whilst successful
Communist candidates become compromisers and heavy-handed
bureaucrats. Those who passed for Labour loyalists, having failed to
sabotage the party from the inside, are rapidly passing over to the
SDP. Persons militant on one topic are conservative over other
issues.

It is this phenomenon that prompted the research that led to the
writing of this book. It occurred to the authors that what was
supposed to be 'progressive' or 'left' was largely self-defined, that
members of a particular organisation happily assumed this title for
themselves, and accordingly defined the others to be of the same
character depending on how close they were to their own outlook.
Communists in particular seemed to be possessors of some sort of
divine right to decide on who were or were not 'Progressive', and to
be able to dismiss their critics as being 'cold-war warriors' or 'anti-
socialist' by their say-so alone. Other sects behave in a not dissimilar
way.

The conclusion of the present study is that 'Right' and 'Left' are
relative, not absolute terms, each depending for its existence upon
the other and defined only in relation to each other. What determines
the true character of an organisation is its reaction to a given concrete
situation. No grouping has the right to arrogate for itself permanent
possession of the fullness of the Socialist tradition. But how, in that
case, are we to assess the claims of these competing organisations? A
good rule of thumb would seem to be to take the Labour and Trade
Union movement as the mainstream, espressing the consensus of
working class political attitudes, and to use that to measure the

tendencies on either side of it. We believe that systematic application of this method yields new and interesting insights into the nature of labour movement politics during the thirties and early forties and, by implication, today as well.

We are all too aware that our unflattering picture of a Communist Party often to the right of Labour flies in the face of the accepted orthodoxy, of right and of left, a good example being Miliband's analysis of *Parliamentary Socialism*. For that reason we have felt it necessary to make frequent and copious use of quotations, deliberately encouraging the protagonists to 'speak for themselves' as far as humanly possible. We realise that they break up the narrative, and we are not insensitive to the irritation that they arouse in the reader, but we can only ask him to bear with us, for they provide the only way open to us to present the relevant material. To the charge that our excerpts are selective we can only reply that, like any other advocate making out a case, we are bound to select only such evidence as casts light upon our theme.

Perhaps the most difficult problem to emerge from this presentation is one that can loosely be described as 'psychological'. How, we may ask, could so many hardworking and courageous men and women, dedicating their whole lives to the emancipation of their fellow workers, be brought to abdicate their critical faculties to the extent of supporting the policies and actions we describe here? The answer of corruption, of 'Moscow gold', in our view is no explanation at all, for even if four pounds a week for a full-timer was riches indeed for a working man at that time, there were limits to the number of full-timers that even the British Communist Party could support. Other reasons must be sought among the rank and file, and we should never forget that it took considerable courage to be a Communist in the twenties and thirties, in a society where every man's hand was against them, where the class war produced more casualties than it does now, and victimisation could bring years of unemployment.

But is it, after all, so difficult for us to understand? The Communist Party and its successor groups still today include the most dedicated working class militants. Being a Communist still brings no social advancement, except perhaps marginally in front organisations or spheres otherwise already dominated by the Party. Yet they continue to turn aside from the struggles before them to cast glazed eyes on some utopia centred upon Moscow, Peking, Pyongyang, Havana or Tirana. The extensive literature of mystication that once surrounded Soviet Russia has since been succeeded by less sophisticated effusions, even to the extent of glorifying a 'Socialist' ruritania in Eastern Europe.[1]

There was much more substance behind the original devotion to the Soviet Union. The Revolution of 1917 was the single most important event of the Twentieth Century, bursting like the sun over a war-torn world with its message of hope, peace and liberation. For the first time in history workers had not only seized power, but held it, against subversion from within and 21 foreign armies from without. The brief flowering of workers' democracy headed by Lenin acted like a magnet to the downtrodden masses of Europe. But the British revolutionaries had already replaced reality with illusion when they forgot Marx's warning that 'the workers have no country' in their enthusiasm for the 'Socialist Fatherland'. And when Stalin's dictatorship reared itself above the bones of Lenin and his companions, the vision outlived by some decades what reality had ever lain beneath it.

The very success of the Russians, compared with the failure of the British revolutionaries, reinforced their dependence on a Marxism developed elsewhere. It was, alas, a Marxism of form rather than of content from the very first. They borrowed all the language of the 'Communist Party', 'Soviets', 'Dictatorship of the Proletariat', 'Democratic Centralism' and the like; making little attempt to relate them to reality either in Russia or in Britain. For Lenin's Communism developed from a differentiation inside Social Democracy, whereas theirs was an amalgam of dogmatic, syndicalist and more or less exotic groups; Lenin's equivalent of a British 'Soviet' was the Leeds Congress, in the mainstream of the movement (with MacDonald, Snowden and the rest of them), not a revolutionary conventicle called out of thin air with a ready-made Russian label. For the 'Dictatorship of the Proletariat' originally meant much more than its purely military aspects, and 'Democratic Centralism' had a real democratic content, not simply a screen for purges and party regimentation, the utter domination of the 'Central Committee' it has come to mean.

The answer to the problem lies in politics and history, not in psychology at all. Almost from its birth British Marxism failed to carry on a meaningful *political* dialogue with the mass working class organisations. It remained a sterile dogma, the self-justification for more or less religious sects, rather than an instrument of critical self-awareness. Its understanding of the wider institutions of the class was limited to a more or less moral denunciation of their leaders, or sermonising over the futility of reforms. Involvement with the

---

1. *Vide* the glossy pamphlet under the title of *Albania: The Most Successful Country in Europe*. It Appeared before the late purges and the 'suicide' of Mehmet Shehu.

actual politics discussed there was minimal, either a counterposition of a dogmatic Marxism to the everyday needs of the movement, or an even more mechanical contrasting of trade union activity with politics. Such education as was attempted centred upon explanations of the Labour Theory of Value, of how the workers were 'robbed at the point of production'. Nothing could be done about it until the 'crisis of capitalism' made everyone discontented and obliged them to turn to the revolutionaries for the key to the way out.

This utopianism of the early British Marxists was really the spiritual reflection of their slim material basis. They accepted a pre-packed Marxism on faith, free not only of contraditions but also of life, which came to them second hand from Moscow, as they had once accepted it lock, stock and barrel from Marx himself (or rather from German Social Democracy). And whilst it might be true that Marx and Lenin 'knew better', the same could not be said for Stalin, Varga or Manuilsky. The inability of the British Marxists to relate *politically* to the life of their own class explains why those who claimed allegiance to the ideas of Marx and Lenin (and later of Trotsky as well) crossed class lines so easily, for they had never worked out properly a political and organisational relationship with the mass movement. Let us recall for a minute the attitude of Marx and Engels to those circles from which the British Communist Party and its latter day imitators sprang. H.M. Hyndman's 'Marxism' was an idiosyncratic growth, repudiated by Marx himself; its first elections were fought accepting Tory money to split the Liberal vote. It condemned the struggle of the Trades Unions; opposed reforms as 'palliatives'; then went on to denounce the Liberal government for not building battleships fast enough, hailed the coming of the First World War with patriotic enthusiasm, and hinted about the dark activities of 'Jewish Princes of Finance'. The war had run two years before the British Socialist Party had dropped its chauvinism—a sad contrast with the semi-pacifist ILP. It comes as no surprise to learn that Engels played a most important rôle in encouraging Bax and Morris' attempt to split the movement before he died; and his preference for the ILP over the SDF when it was formed has been fully justified by subsequent history.

The groups that succeeded the SDF-British Socialist Party were little improvement, and their stamp upon the Communist Party and its modern Trotskyist and Maoist imitators has remained to this day. One of the founding organisations of the CPGB was an ex-syndicalist organisation, openly hostile to Marxism; another's hatred of the Labour Party was notorious. Even by today's student politics standards Sylvia Pankhurst's group would be considered 'far left'.

It was not that they were lacking in judgment, or courage, or sincerity, or even in involvement with the labour movement as such. The list of the founding leaders of the Communist Party reads like a gazeteer of the most capable contemporary and future trade union militants. But the strategic *political* task, their orientation to the Labour Party and the political plane in general, found them sadly lacking. The BSP alone had finally affiliated to the Labour Party a couple of years or so earlier: but it had earned the hostility of all the other groups for so doing, and its political errors during the war had been more deadly than those of the others. Its relations with the Labour Party, in fact, provided one of the chief sources of division from the very beginning, and considerably delayed the formation of a united party, which would not have come about without the intervention of the Russians through the Communist International. We can well sympathise with Lenin's immense labours to unify these squabbling groups and get them to accept the necessity for political action at all, let alone Labour Party affiliation!

Such were the roots of the British Communist Party, and they go far to explain what follows in these pages. All its vices were present at birth, in its tenuous understanding of the movement of the class, its false and one-sided counterposition of trade union militancy and political action, its penchant for replacing politics with intrigue, and in the sectarianism that expressed itself in the vilification of those closest to it.[2] Here (again) we are aware that we are challenging accepted orthodoxies, whether in Challinor's attempt to discover 'Bolshevism' in the semi-syndicalist SLP, or Kendall's theory of a healthy revolutionary movement emerging out of all these grouplets, which was side-tracked by the Russian Revolution.

That is not to say that there does not exist a Marxist critique of the British labour movement, but it does not come out of these traditions. Was it not Engels who foresaw the working class' next step—the formation of a broad-based independent political party of Labour? Was it not he who welcomed the foundation of the ILP, that was to make such a contribution to bringing it about? Was it not Lenin who seconded the amendment that brought the British Labour Party into the Second International, and who, many years later, demanded the affiliation of the Communist Party to the Labour Party?[3] Was it not the Communist International that defined the concrete form of the struggle for the Worker's United Front in Britain as the fight to gain the acceptance of the Communists into the

---

2. It is nonsense to explain this by Stalinism, as some do. The treatment of A. J. Cook and others had been meted out already to such as M. Phillips Price and Raymond Postgate, long before 'Stalinisation' had a chance to set in.

Labour Party? And finally, did not Trotsky demand the entry of his supporters into that party, as the realisation 'from inside' of the unity of the revolutionaries and the workers?

If we take these things together, they amount to an entirely different picture of the problem of the relationship between revolutionaries and the mass organisations of the class, and they agree with the picture of the general development of revolutionary parties in historical experience. Except in lands where there was no party of the workers already in existence, there has never been a revolutionary party created out of recruiting in ones and twos to a sect. Lenin's own organisation was the Majority section of the Russian Social Democratic Labour Party. All the mass parties of the Third International sprang from splits inside previously existing Social Democratic movements. The principle even extends into the Trotskyist movement, which as a whole never attained mass status. Two out of three of their groups that did attain it for a short while (in Vietnam and Sri Lanka) did so because their ultimate organisational split with the Stalinist Communists did not come until as late as 1939. The other example (Bolivia) is no real exception, for before the rise of the Trotskyists there did not exist a mass party of the workers of any sort in that country.

In Britain the problem of where revolutionary parties come from is further complicated by the almost unique structure of the labour movement in general. In other countries, the working class party existed first, and then founded trade unions as its extensions; or trades unions existed completely divorced from political life. Those countries in which the political party and the trades unions are intimately united at every level are so through a more or less conscious imitation of the British example. The main mistake of left wingers for the last eighty years lies in attempting to pose a division between trades unionism and reformist politics, justifying their belonging to the unions, but denouncing the Labour Party from outside. But the British labour movement is unitary, almost monolithic. Co-operatives, a few Socialist Societies, and the manual trades unions are all united with each other through the agency of the Labour Party. This is not only the case with annual conference and the 'block vote', but stretches down to the very bones of the movement in the localities. Trade unions send delegates to local parties: political resolutions are passed over to them for discussion, once they have gone through the local union branch. The consciousness that this creates in the activists and rank and file admits

---

3.   Against the will of its sectarian leaders who, may we add, did their level best to sabotage it from the very first.

of no division, no Chinese Wall, between 'politics' and 'trade union activity'. Political, reformist, activity in parliament or the local arena are simply the political equivalent of the struggle for higher wages and better working conditions in the trade union. Any contradiction between them exists mainly in the minds of left sectarians. The British Labour Party and the trades unions have to be approached as a unitary phenomenon, or as allied concepts; and from *inside*.

There is another consideration that applies, even if this particular structure of British working class politics did not exist. Such are the conditions of survival under capitalism, that the working class requires class-wide (and massive) institutions to defend itself. Apart from their natural (and entirely positive) loyalty towards institutions painfully built up over generations at great cost in effort and self-sacrifice, if workers left their organisations every time their leaders betrayed them, they would have no fundamental defences at all. A multitude of 'pure', 'revolutionary' or 'militant' unions would exist, with minuscule following and no bargaining position at all. The worker would be at the mercy of every employer. The workers' loyalty to such highly insensitive unions as the EEPTU lies at the heart of the realisation that a large institution, however compromised, however often it betrays, is some defence, but a small one, however militant, is of no use at all. Working class politics (like Marxism itself) are unitary.

Because of the way it was founded, and its intimate connection with the trade unions, the Labour Party also enjoys this relationship with the working class. The disappointments of each successive Labour Government do not lead to a mass exodus into the ranks of the Communist Party (and still less of the SWP or the IMG) not because they distrust the motives of these groupings (though that may be the case in individual instances), but simply because they plainly do not possess the potential to transform themselves into mass organisations, and therefore are of no use to them in the present circumstances.

That does not mean that workers remain satisfied with their leaders or their institutions, but it does mean that when they sense their inadequacy their first inclination is to attempt, not to discard them outright, but to reform them from within. A tool is not generally discarded until it has been well tested and found badly wanting, whereas ideas can be picked up and dropped at will. That alone explains why the left wing sects are mainly middle class, and the workers' organisations are mainly reformist.

Without this sort of analysis, many features of the behaviour of the British labour movement remain inexplicable. There is no other way of understanding the pattern of the flow of interest between the trades unions at one time, then back to the Labour Party at another. When the limitations of purely trade union activity show themselves, then attention shifts to the task of electing a Labour Government. When this shows its inability to take the movement forward, then hopes become centred on the trades unions. When we apply the alternating pattern to the politics of this century—Labour Government followed by General Strike, and then Labour Government again, just to take the example of the twenties alone— we must realise that it is the same people who are expressing their social aspirations in these seemingly different institutions. The period we have selected for this little book is a classic example, showing how the rising militancy in the unions towards the end of the Second World War was soon reflected in the most radical Labour Government that has yet come to office.

Lack of understanding among those who called themselves Marxists of this relationship has condemned British Marxism to sterility. It lies at the root of the fact that the technical vocabulary of Marxism (apart from its economics, for obvious reasons) is either German, or Russian, but not English. British Marxism has never been able to take on a life of its own, for it has carried on no dialogue with the working class *as a whole*. Even today it exists as the private preserve of university academics, of the immense growth industry in 'Labour History', cheerfully harnessed to the task of gaining lectureships and professorial chairs, rather than the self-emancipation of working people. Marxism has become its opposite—a means of advancement in the academic world, a branch of literary criticism, an enjoyable exercise in abstract philosophy, a colourful antiquarian investigation of the lower reaches of society, all the more jargon-ridden as it becomes abstruse. The task of our modern philosophers is not to explain the world, but to confuse it. The task of changing it never arises.

For this reason Marxism has turned into its opposite, transformed from a guide to action into a theology of contemplation. But this change was long under way before the rise of our modern academic Marxists, and they are no more to blame for it than 'the Russians'. Long before the influence of Russia or of Stalin, British revolutionaries were quoting Marx as an oracle, reducing his ideas to the Labour Theory of Value alone, or further dogmatising them through the writings of Daniel de Leon. They were already accustomed to pre-packed analyses provided for them by august authorities, and it was natural for them to look from Germany to Soviet Russia, and from Marx to Lenin as the fount of all wisdom. Future progress from Stalin to Mao Tse-Tung, Fidel Castro, or Enver Hoxha was no less natural. But Russian patriotism could so easily develop into British...

This little book is not, and has no pretensions to be, a history of the Communist Party during these years. For this readers are referred to the standard works by Pelling and Dewar, which give as good a summary as is possible, given the refusal of the Communist Party authorities to allow access to their internal material by all but specially authorised students. Nor do the present writers look forward to the results of the Party's own historians, if previous examples of their work are anything to go by.

The aim of the present sketch is to concentrate upon one historical problem alone: why, during the decade 1935-45, did the Communist Party fail to replace the Labour Party at the head of the British working class? Why, at a period of radicalisation of the working class in western Europe, when huge Communist Parties grew in France, Spain and Italy, did their British cousins end the period with no more influence in the labour movement than they had at the beginning?

The question is not a matter of historical interest alone. Impressed with the success of their continental co-thinkers, contrasted with their own impotence, the leaders of the British Communist Party proclaim their adherence to 'Eurocommunism', and look back to the war time and the years of the 'Popular Front' as their golden age. But the evidence is overwhelming that it was their policy during this time that sacrificed, perhaps forever, any chance they had of replacing the Labour Party in the hearts of the British workers.

This investigation makes no false claims to impartiality, but is written from a very definite point of view, that of members of the Labour Party who see the relevance of Marxist methods. It seeks to show that the reason for Communists' failure was not that they stood generally to the *left* of the mass movement, but on its *right*. The violent changes of line that placed them in this position sprang from the foreign policy requirements of the Soviet state. In presenting the answer in this way, we are (obviously) passing no judgments upon the personal motives of the rank and file member of the party, who is often the most earnest supporter of what he understands as the cause of the working class, both then and now, any more than we are endorsing the motives of the Labour leaders, in rejecting their overtures. For the growth or decline of political parties is rooted in the development of social and political events, not in individual psychology; and past history shows that it is in times of crisis that the working class starts to question its political allegiance and begins to consider changing it. The aim of this study is to find out why this did *not* happen.

Study has its own rewards, though changing circumstances is not generally one of them. But those who lay claim to historical materialism do not investigate history 'for its own sake', but for the lessons it affords for the future struggle of the working class. A slump has come again, this time creating four million unemployed. Again, the trades unions and the Labour Party are in retreat. Already one union, ASLEF, fighting alone, has been forced to its knees, with the connivance of the TUC. The Labour Party itself, having lost much of its credibility, has suffered a right-wing split in its parliamentary group. Time alone can tell whether it will tread in the steps of Ramsay MacDonald or of Oswald Mosley.

Meanwhile, the left is no better armed theoretically than it was in the thirties. Those who claim to be revolutionaries still show little embarassment at going on 'peace' rallies with Liberals and clerics, and Communists project their economic 'alternative' in terms of the preservation of British interests.

Is it too much to hope that this account will not only show whence these policies come, but also their inevitable result, which is more to the point?

Short as this book has turned out to be (and it is longer than we desired or expected), it has not been brought together without considerable background research, of grubbing in the archives, of sorting through masses of documents and newspapers. Foremost in our thanks must go to Jim Ring, Bill Thompson and Clarence Chrysostom, without whose help it could never have appeared. Their solid, plodding work behind the scenes has made it a co-operative effort, not an individual endeavour, in that way resembling its theme.

In the same way our personal judgment has been constantly modified. Without the continued guidance and support of Reg and Daisy Groves, Roy Tearse, Selvaraj and many others, there would be more errors in this book, both in fact and in interpretation, than have turned out now. Where the writers have disregarded their advice, it has not been done lightly, but it does absolve them of any responsibility for the book's contents. The mistakes are ours alone.

Anyone who has the rashness to approach this subject can only do so with considerable wider help and constant encouragement. The people who have furnished information, advice, documents. etc, are legion. We hope that it will not be counted a discourtesy to all the others if we name just a few—Margaret Kentfield, John Robinson, Jock Haston, Harry Wicks—who, we might add, would disagree with many of the statements we have made. We hope that we have not stretched their tolerance too far.

Sadly, Hugo Dewar's death on 14th June last year makes it impossible for us to extend our thanks to him also.

27th August 1982

Chapter One

The Field of Battle: The situation in 1934

1934 saw a year of defeat for Communism on a world scale. In China the Kiangsi-Hunan soviet had been eliminated by Chiang Kai-Shek, and the Chinese Communist Party had escaped annihilation only by the sacrifice of four fifths of its army on 'The Long March'. In Austria the labour movement had been smashed when Dollfüss turned the artillery on the workers' flats. A similar result followed for the Spanish working class when the army put down the Asturian Commune. The German workers had lain prostrate and numb under the rule of Hitler for two years.

Whilst not responsible for all these defeats (the Austrian and Spanish Communist Parties were quite small), Communist policy had been greatly to blame in the most spectacular of them. During the previous 'Third Period' of the Communist International's history the world labour movement had been divided by a frenzied sectarianism. Socialists had been denounced as 'Social Fascists', and Communists had been directed to concentrate their attacks on them, instead of upon bourgeois enemies; trade unions were split up or split off in an attempt to form pure 'revolutionary' unions; in the East peasant uprisings were ordered on the basis of very little support; and against a backcloth of fratricidal antagonism, reaching so deep into society as to cause playground fights between the children of Socialists and Communists, Hitler had come to power without a blow being struck.

This suicidal orientation would have caused the utter destruction of the Communist movement, if it had continued. The rapid drop in Communist Party membership on three continents bore witness to that. Only the complete regimentation of the Comintern can explain why it was ever accepted at all.

For the policy had its origin in purely Russian conditions. A grain strike there had made it necessary to begin the forced collectivisation of peasant land and the 'liquidation of the kulaks as a class', which in turn meant the removal of their protectors within the government, the Bukharin group. Since the conduct of the affairs of the Communist International had been left to Bukharin (after the removal of Zinoviev) he in turn had to be removed as a 'rightist' by a campaign for 'left' policies within it. The new orientation had been lent credibility by the misery spread across the world by the Wall Street Crash, which the official economists analysed as the final collapse of capitalism. Attacks against other labour movement institutions could be justified as a 'class against class' assault, one last heave to bring down the rotten and tottering structures of the bourgeois world. By 1934 the whole policy was at a dead end. The world Communist movement was on the edge of ruin. And with the rise of Hitler, the German-Soviet relationship under the Rapallo system was also defunct, leaving the Soviet Union dangerously isolated among the world powers.

And whereas some of the Communist Parties on the continent might have some fat to lose, the British party was already skin and bone. By the end of 1934 it had less than six thousand members, largely on paper, of which a high percentage were unemployed. Nor was this surprising. It had gone out of its way to alienate any outside support of any sort. A. J. Cook, their friend for many a year, had been dismissed 'with the contempt that he deserves';[1] and the further left any politicians stood in the mass movement, the more violently they were denounced as 'the prop of MacDonald and the worst enemies of the working class'.[2] Fenner Brockway in particular was singled out as 'an unscrupulous agent of the Social Fascists'.[3]

The leftism of the CPGB did not stop at words. They had split the Tailors and Garment Workers' Union by founding another, the United Clothing Workers, and the Miners by setting up the United Mineworkers of Scotland. An attempt to do the same in South Wales foundered against the opposition of Arthur Horner, one of their own supporters, who was too locally entrenched to be moved without wrecking their organisational strength in the industry. As the United Clothing Workers were limited to London, and the UMS to Fife, the policy also threatened to split up the trade unions on a regional basis. Fortunately, the damage that the policy could have done was limited by the small numbers and even less influence of the party.

They were rapidly gaining a bad name for deliberate acts of hooliganism. When two members of the General Council of the TUC came down to speak in support of the leader of the Tailors' and Garment Workers' Union, they were shouted down, with the justification that

'The workers will not give any such "free speech" to these swindlers and lickspittlers. Let the workers all over the country follow the example of the London Clothing Workers and hound the leaders of the Labour Party and the reactionary trade union leaders off the platform'.[4]

Attacks upon Labour Party public meetings along these lines followed in Poplar and Battersea,[5] where George Lansbury, by no means 'one of the worst of the Labour leaders', was prevented from speaking by the orchestrated shouting and singing of the Communists. Such actions led some sections of the trade union movement to raise seriously the question of providing their meetings with the means to ensure their right to be heard.[6]

The inspiration for this sort of behaviour was a propaganda atmosphere of scare mongering and hysteria. The *Daily Worker* for Saturday 19th March, 1932 went out under the headline of "War Menaces You", and then went on to announce that "World War has begun".

It was fortunate for the British Communists that this policy was about to be changed, though they lacked the means to initiate that change themselves. Again, the alteration came from the foreign policy needs of the Soviet Union.

To begin with, Stalin had gravely underestimated the nature of the Nazi threat to the Soviet Union. He expected that the Rapallo system of friendly Soviet-German relations would continue, since Hitler had openly announced his intention to revise the Treaty of Versailles, which could force Germany more into the arms of the USSR by worsening relations with France and Britain. By renewing the Treaty of Berlin in May 1933 (one of the economic agreements that followed the Rapallo policy) Stalin had been, in effect, the first foreign head of state to accept the legality of the new Nazi regime. As Litvinov was still saying at the end of the year, 'our relations with Germany are determined not by its internal but its external policy'.[7]

But it did not take long for Hitler's foreign policy intentions to become as clear as his domestic operations. In January 1934 he signed a non-aggression pact with Poland, whose only purpose was to secure his flank against the Soviet Union, leaving him free to make what pickings he could elsewhere. The bad relations between Poland and Russia underlined the fundamental hostility of Germany and pointed clearly to a major alteration in the foreign policy of the new state. It was clear that Soviet foreign affairs were in for a new alignment, and the world Communist movement was heading for another zigzag.

A diplomatic drive began now for alliance with France, and through France, with Britain. In September 1934 the Soviet Union entered the League of Nations, condemned by Lenin as a 'thieves' den'. It meant support by the USSR for the Versailles system. involving alliance with one group of world powers against the other. In May 1935 the French diplomat, Pierre Laval, was in Moscow to sign a mutual aid pact against either state being attacked by a 'European Power', and with this went approval of French re-armament plans. As an official communiqué issued on the 16th May expressed it,

> 'Stalin expressed complete understanding and approval of the national defence policy pursued by France with the object of maintaining armed forces at the level consistent with its security requirements'.[8]

Long before the Seventh World Congress of the Comintern met to ratify the new policy of the "Popular Front" in August 1935, the line was in operation among the Communist Parties abroad, showing how careless the Russians were becoming at preserving the outward forms of a revolutionary international. When it was accepted without a murmur, it showed also how submissive the national sections were becoming to the diplomatic requirements of the Soviet state. The task of the parties in Western Europe now became to form blocs, not only with the 'Social Fascist' parties of the Second International, but with radicals, Liberals, and even 'democratic' nationalists, to put pressure upon (or form) governments in those states marked out as 'democratic', 'peace loving' and 'anti-Fascist'. In France it was necessary to include Radicals and Radical Socialists to overcome the Socialists' traditional pacifism (what use was France as an ally to the USSR without an army?), and in Britain it was necessary to include Liberals and Tories to prevent an outbreak of anti-imperialist feeling in a Labour/CP alliance. For what use was Britain to the USSR without its imperial power?

The new 'Popular Front' Policy was launched at an auspicious moment for the Comintern. The working class of Western Europe was acutely conscious of the fact that Hitler, Dollfüss and Lerroux had got away with the damage they had done because of the disunity of the labour movement in their respective countries. Sentiment for unity was flowing strongly. It only remained to be determined—unity with whom—and for what?

The necessity for unity between different sections of the working class movement had long been understood, by none better than Marxists who accepted the need for the organisation of separate vanguard parties. Long ago in the *Communist Manifesto* it had been affirmed that Communists had 'no separate interests from the interests of the proletariat in general', were setting up 'no sectarian principles on which they wish to model the proletarian movement', but who 'represent always the interests of the movement as a whole'.[9] This insight sprang from the understanding of the basic underlying unity of interests of the working class as a whole which Communists alone possessed, as opposed to the different political parties, trade unions, etc., that stood for sectional interests or for various privileged or semi-privileged layers within it. For the point at which the working class becomes a class for itself is the point at which it realises its unity, and begins a political struggle, i.e. for power:

> 'Economic conditions had first transformed the mass of the people of the country into workers. The domination of capital has created for this mass a common situation, common interests. This mass is thus already a class as against capital, but not yet for itself. In the struggle, of which we have pointed out only a few phases, this mass becomes united, and constitutes itself as a class for itself. The interests it defends become class interests. But the struggle of class against class is a political struggle.'[10]

The problem of the relations between the revolutionaries and the mass working class movement had been further explored by the Communist International itself during and following its Third World Congress. Its main slogan was interpreted as requiring 'the Communist Parties and the Communist International as a whole *to support the slogan of the united front of the workers* and to take the initiative in this matter'.[11] In the case of Britain the Labour Party was defined as 'a kind of general workers' organisation for the entire country', into which it was the task of British Communists 'to begin a vigorous campaign for their acceptance', employing the slogan of 'the revolutionary united front against the capitalists'.[12] Blocs with non-working class forces (as opposed to temporary or episodic agreements for particular purposes) were denounced. Indeed,

> 'one of the most reliable methods of counteracting inside the working class the moods and ideas of the "Left Bloc", i.e., a bloc between the workers and a certain section of the bourgeoisie against another section of the bourgeoisie, is through promoting persistently and resolutely the idea of a *bloc between all the sections of the working class against the whole bourgeoisie*'.[13]

The policy of the Popular Front ran counter to all this, with its aim of linking the working class movement with bourgeois parties and politicians, though the term 'United Front' was used to describe it, especially during the earliest period.[14] In British terms, (as we shall see), it meant a return to the 'Lib-Lab.' politics of the time before the rise of Labour as an independent party, running directly counter to the traditions accumulated by the British working class during half a century of struggle.

Not only past tradition stood in its way, but recent experience. The working class movement by 1934 was only just beginning to recover from the blow it had received from such an inter-class alliance, and was in no mood to enter another one. Official spokesmen had explained the failure of the first two Labour governments by their minority position in parliament, inhibiting them from taking more forthright steps and making them dependent upon the Liberals for their survival.[15] The National Government of 1931 included Liberals and Conservatives along with a 'National Labour' component led by Ramsay Macdonald, Phillip Snowden and Jimmy Thomas, which had cut the dole in the middle of the slump 'in the national interest'. The onslaught of this multi-class bloc in the General Election of 1931 had cost Labour 236 seats and cut their parliamentary presence to 51. The unity of the movement was further weakened by the decision of the ILP at a special conference in July 1932 to disaffiliate from the Labour Party.

The need to repair its bruised limbs and defend itself against an alliance of all its enemies led to a deeper feeling for class unity in Labour's ranks, and a corresponding shift to the Left. The Manifesto on which the Party fought the election of 1931 called for the nationalisation of banking and credit, and the organisation of the basic industries and public services under national ownership.[16] The annual conference of 1932 accepted a motion from the Socialist League calling for a General Strike in the event of war, and an amendment to nationalise the joint stock banks. The document presented by the NEC in July 1934 talked about an effective share by the workers in the direction of industry, along with the nationalisation of the banks, transport, water, coal, electricity, agriculture, iron and steel, engineering etc. Nor was this the usual liturgical recital of faith in the Socialist cause that surfaces only at conference time. The Executive Report to the Conference of 1932 asked for a Labour Government 'with effective authority to proceed boldly and speedily with its programme of contructive socialism',[17] and Trevelyan's resolution calling for a future Labour government immediately on assuming office to promulgate 'definite socialist legislation' went through without even the formality of a vote.[18]

When Henderson attempted to oppose it he was all but shouted down, and even Attlee, who seconded, had to admit that 'the events of the last year have shown that no further progress can be made in seeking to get crumbs from the rich man's table'. Not long afterwards he began to talk about the possibility of Labour passing an enabling act after coming into office to take over the commanding heights of the economy.

The truth was that Labour had moved to its furthest Left position (up to 1945), while still retaining its old relationship with the working class. The ILP, down to 7,166 members, and the Communist Party, at 5,800, ranked at no more than a temporary irritant—from the 5 members of the ILP in Parliament and from Communist agitation among the unemployed. The catastrophic fall in the number of Labour MPs was hardly in proportion to its loss of votes (some 1.7 million), which still amounted to more than it had in 1924, and its relations with the trades unions and the mass of working class voters remained unimpaired. And slowly, and painfully, it began to regain its lost ground. Already in the municipal elections of 1932 Labour had won over half the council seats in the largest towns; and further gains in the following year gave Labour majorities to 25 councils. Labour took control of the LCC in March 1934, and in the November local elections gained 457 seats in London and control of 15 Metropolitan boroughs. In the provinces 41 boroughs were under Labour control.

The same picture came out clearly in parliamentary by-elections. At East Fulham on October 25th 1933 the Labour candidate turned a Tory majority of 14,521 in 1931 into a Labour majority of 3,516. At Liverpool Wavertree early in the following year the Labour candidate even exceeded the votes gained in 1929. Neither at East Fulham, where the Communists had called upon the electors to spoil their ballot papers by writing 'Communist' across them, nor at North Hammersmith, where Ted Bramley had gained a derisory 614 votes in an attempt to split the working class vote, were the CP able to make an impression on this rise of class feeling. The tide was flowing strongly back to Labour, which was to give them 154 seats on a poll of 8½ million in the General Election of November 1935.

The recovery of the political influence of the movement was mirrored by the progress of the trades unions. Total membership climbed from its lowest point in the inter-war years in 1933 of 4,392,000 to 4,867,000 by 1935. All over the country the Communist-led National Unemployed Workers' Movement gathered demonstrations and marches, serious strikes broke out among Lancashire weavers and London busmen, and a series of local disputes showed that the working class was recovering its will to resist.

Buttressed by this feeling from below, the Labour leaders had every expectation sooner or later of forming a government by themselves, and were in no mood to compromise, either with the declining Liberals, split three ways between the followers of Sir John Simon, Sir Herbert Samuel and Lloyd George, or their deadly enemies the Tories, or even with the rising star of the Communists. In September 1933 William Gillies published an official pamphlet called *The Communist Solar System*, which exposed the local operations of the front groups, elaborated for the Comintern and its sections into a system of amazing complexity by the genius of Willi Muenzenberg. The policy of the People's Front was to run up against a movement that was more united and determined than ever before.

Footnotes

1 R. Palme Dutt, 'Cook: Break with the Revolutionary Working Class; Editorial Reply', in *Labour Monthly*, vol. xi, no. 6, June 1929, p. 34.
2 R. Palme Dutt, 'War on the Labour Government! Capitalism's Shield Against Workers' Attacks—Smash this Barrier', in the *Daily Worker*, January 1st 1930, p.20. 'The more the Labour Party embarks on its open Social Fascist course the more dangerous become the "Lefts", the most dangerous enemies of the revolutionary proletariat within the working-class movement'.
3 'Sham Lefts Wire to India Seeking for Allies in National Congress. Remove Brockway', in the *Daily Worker*, 2nd January, 1930.
4 Editorial, 'Free Speech', in the *Daily Worker*, January 22nd 1930.
5 'Poplar Workers' Anger', in the *Daily Worker*, 8th April, 1930; Editorial, 'Lido Lansbury', in the *Daily Worker*, 28th September 1930; 'Lansbury Shouted Down', in the *Daily Worker*, 25th November 1930. Reg Groves recalls that the Communists had official instructions to break up the Battersea meeting—Conversation with Al Richardson, 23rd August 1979.
6 *Cf.* A. M. Wall (Secretary of the London Trades Council): 'Steps are being taken by the trades unions to defend free speech in the London area', *Daily Herald*, 21st January 1930.
7 J. Degras (ed.), *Soviet Documents on Foreign Policy*, vol. iii, p. 56.
8 *Op. cit*, pp. 131-2.
9 *Communist Manifesto*, SLP edition, 1909, pp. 15-16.
10 Marx, *The Poverty of Philosophy*, Progress Publishers, Moscow, 1976, pp. 159-160.
11 ECCI, 'Directives on the United Front of the Workers and on the Attitudes to Workers Belonging to the Second, Two-and-a-Half, and Amsterdam Internationals, and to Those Who Support Anarcho-Syndicalist Organisations', in H. Gruber, *International Communism in The Era of Lenin*, New York, 1972, p. 321.

12 *Op. cit,* p. 323.
13 L. Trotsky, 'On the United Front' (theses accepted by the Enlarged Plenum of the ECCI, February, 1922), in *The First Five Years of the Communist International.* New Park, 1974, vol. ii, pp. 103-4.
14 The Popular Front went under various guises, names and transformations. From the previous politics it was often called the 'United Front'; then the 'Peoples' Front', and 'United Peace Alliance', etc. The term by which it is now generally known is a more or less accurate translation from the French 'front populaire', as being the more well-known example of it.
15 *Cf.* The Election Manifesto of 1931: 'the intolerable restrictions of its minority position in the House of Commons', *Annual Conference Report 1932*, pp. 319-22.
16 *Op.cit, ibid.*
17 *Op. cit,* p. 4.
18 *Op. cit,* pp. 204ff.

Chapter Two

Left Right,
Right Left,
1934-5

The process by which the British Communist Party changed its line was a very uneven one. It was not a question of the incompetence of the local leadership, as was to be common later on when they found difficulty in keeping in step with Moscow; in this case they were only reflecting the confusion that prevailed right up to the highest circles of the Comintern. So stunned were the Communist leaders at the coming to power of Hitler, that for a while they refused to believe the evidence of their own ears. As late as June 1933 they were still saying that 'only defeatists and open opportunists can talk about the working class being beaten in the struggle against fascism, or its having 'lost a battle' and 'suffered a defeat',[1] and that 'the KPD is not only undestroyed, but its influence on the masses is greater than ever'.[2] In addition, the previous 'Third Period' line of 'Social Fascism' had not been without its ambiguities. Though the Communists had been instructed to attack the Social Democratic leaders under this slogan, they had also been told to try and construct the 'United Front from Below' with the Social Democratic masses. The impossibility of carrying out these two policies simultaneously had led to a peculiar situation of blowing hot and cold.

For example, in Britain the unemployed movement was not supposed to be a purely party body, and it had proved impossible to keep ILP leaders from participating in its deputations and demonstrations. After Maxton and Kirkwood had been involved in the deputation to MacDonald in September 1931, the Central Committee meeting in the following December had criticised this as 'a sign of opportunist tendencies in the party'.[3] But it was manifest absurdity to claim that such bodies were not party organisations, and yet complain when persons from other parties got mixed up with them.

From time to time it was necessary to save face by making unity appeals 'for the record', to shift the blame for these splits onto the shoulders of the Social Democrats. When Hitler assumed his dictatorial powers in March 1933 the Executive Committee of the Communist International instructed its national sections to approach their opposite numbers of the Socialist International with proposals for joint action, and for the meantime 'during the time of a common fight against capitalism and fascism to refrain from making attacks on Social Democratic organisations'.[4] The British Communists wrote to the Labour Party, ILP, TUC and Co-op Party to consider plans for joint activity.[5] The Labour Party on March 22nd, 1933 replied with an abrupt refusal to meet either the CP or the ILP, and the Hastings Conference of the Party denounced the association of its members with Communist 'front' groups. The Labour Party clearly meant business, and the unpopularity of the Communist's sectarianism enabled the EC to get the support of the following annual conference at Southport in 1934 to give it power to take disciplinary action against those who broke this ban by the overwhelming vote of 1,820,000 to 89,000. At the same time the TUC had sent a circular round its affiliated unions on relations with the Communists.[6] The famous 'black circular' of October 1934 forbade trades councils to accept Communists as delegates and requested the unions to bar them from office. The General Council of the TUC adopted it as policy in March 1935, and asked trades councils and trades unions to modify their rules accordingly. The following conference of September 1935 ratified the position of the General Council by a vote of 1,869,000 to 1,274,000.

The unreality of the Communist's new approach appeared in a report given by Harry Pollitt to a meeting of the Executive Committee of the Communist International on December 20th, 1934:

'We are proposing that in places where the CP, ILP and Labour Party are all putting forward candidates, an attempt be made to reach agreement on the candidate who can best express the united front desires of the workers. For this we propose a Workers' Selection Conference should be held; let the three candidates be voted upon at that conference, and a workers' candidate be selected on the basis of the united front. Should the Labour Party refuse and we have reached an agreement with the ILP and if the Labour candidate had the least chance in the election, we should propose to them that they withdraw their candidate from the field.'

After that he added generously that if there was still a chance of a 'capitalist' candidate getting in on a split vote, the ILP/CP should be prepared to withdraw their opposition to Labour. The spectacle of the tiny British Communist Party dictating to Labour how it should select its candidates was a flight of fancy unequalled since Lewis Carroll.

For what the Communists had in mind for Labour was not a unity of the working class forces, but one across class lines with sections of the establishment. For example, inspired by the Communists, the Abertillery Trades Council, in 'united front' with the shopkeepers and the local churches, appealed to the TUC for action on unemployment.[7] The National Joint Council (later to be the National Council of Labour) had already anticipated this when it laid down that

> 'The real "United Front" is that formed by the Trades Union Congress, the Labour Party and the Co-operative Movement, and the place for sincere advocates of "unity" is inside these movements.'[8]

But the Popular Front campaign of the Communists was by now in full swing, having received the official ratification of the Seventh Congress of the Comintern in August 1935. It called for a 'united front' (sic) with 'mass national liberation, religious–democratic and pacifist organisations and their adherents'.[9]

The way to a Popular Front in Britain lay through affiliation to the Labour Party, and through that to alliances further to the right. Propaganda adjustments had to be made. The February Conference of the CP had still entitled its programme *'For Soviet Britain'*. But when Pollitt reported to the London District Committee in October 1935 it was replaced by the slogan 'For a Labour Government'. As a conciliatory gesture the CP now withdrew all the candidates it was putting up against Labour in the general election of 14th November, 1935, with the exception of two—Pollitt, who was defeated, and Gallacher, who was successful. At the end of November the CP asked for affiliation to the Labour Party for the first time since the 20's, to be met with the NEC's blank refusal. A massive campaign was mounted to reverse this at the following annual conference of the Party. As a first step 'in the interests of unity' the party wound up its split unions among the clothing-workers and the Scots miners at the end of 1935. The CP now began to appeal to those who stood on Labour's right. A Conference of Peace and Friendship with the USSR held in London on December 7th and 8th attracted 60 representatives of 'peace societies', 25 from religious bodies (including Dr. Maude Royden, Methodist, and greetings from the Bishop of London) and luminaries of science, politics and tradition from all across the political spectrum, from Professor Blackett and Bob Boothby to Viscount Hastings and Lord Listowel.

It could hardly appeal to those who were regaining their faith in the Labour Party from a class point of view, and must have assisted Transport House in rejecting the unity policy of the Communists. Of course, the Labour Party NEC were by no means averse to hobnobbing with respectable people themselves, and their attitude sprang from their own suspicions towards the unity of the labour movement, even by the inclusion of the small Communist Party, and their rejection of all forms of struggle outside the ballot box. But they were able to make political capital out of the feeling for unity by pointing to the split in the German labour movement as a major cause of Hitler's success. As the National Council of Labour put it in *Democracy Versus Dictatorship*, 'masses of the working class electors—divided between Communism and Social Democracy—had fallen victims to Fascism'.

They were well ahead of the Communists' understanding of the matter. A year later Gallacher was still denouncing 'the apparently simple, but totally un-Marxian solution of a united front with Social Democracy on a basis agreeable to Social Democracy, with the main object of keeping out the fascists'.[10] Other party spokesmen tried to claim that Communism bore no responsibility for the disunity at all. 'It is not true that the German Communists split the ranks of the proletariat in struggle against the capitalists', affirmed Andrew Rothstein. 'On the contrary, while organising the united front from below—of the rank-and-file, whatever their political creed—they repeatedly offered to come to an agreement with the Social Democratic leaders as well . . .'[11]

Moreover, Labour leaders were justified in their suspicion of the motives of the Communists. The Thirteenth Plenum of the Executive Committee of the Communist International of December 1933 was still demanding a fight against Social Democracy and its 'hypocritical and treacherous sophistries',and a year after Hitler's assumption of power the only way to form the United Front was still 'by fighting relentlessly to destroy the treacherous Second International'.[12] Throughout this 'for the record' unity drive 'the fight against the Social Democratic poison',[13] went on against those who 'only object to being called by their proper name—Social Fascists',[14] justified by Gallacher on the grounds that

'There is nothing irreconcilable between Social Democracy and Fascism; on the contrary, Social Democracy can accept everything which Fascism does'.[15]

The fact that Social Democrats and Communists were side by side accepting what Fascism was doing to them in the concentration camps did not disturb his logic; any more than appealing to one set of 'fascists' for support in the fight against another had disturbed the logic of the Communist International.

Approaches to the ILP met with more success, though even here the operation could not be carried out without clumsiness and a certain credibility gap.

The experience of the Second Labour Government had been a disillusioning one for the ILP. Criticism of the complete failure of the administration to deal with unemployment, and the subsequent betrayal of MacDonald, Snowden and Thomas had set up a rapid reaction to the left among the ILP's members. At the same time the tightening of discipline in Labour's ranks had meant the assertion of the parliamentary whip over the ILP's MPs, bringing them into conflict with ILP policy as expressed by its annual conference. During the autumn 1931 general election the Labour Party executive had refused endorsement to the 19 ILP candidates. After prolonged negotiations with the Labour Leaders a special conference of the ILP meeting in Bradford in July 1932 had decided to disaffiliate by a vote of 241 votes to 142.

The split had taken place over the relationship between the ILP parliamentary group and their own party on the one side, and the rest of the Labour group in the House of Commons on the other. But it was widely interpreted among the rank and file—even the leadership[16]—as a move to the left on the ILP's part, a break with the reformist traditions of the Labour Party and a move towards a revolutionary position. The underlying cause was the tremendous strain placed on the relationship between the activists of the Labour movement and their leaders by the ignominious failure of the Labour Party to cope with the agony of unemployment.

The argument to disaffiliate from the Labour Party at the previous annual conference of the ILP in Easter 1932 had been led by Dr. C. K. Cullen and Jack Gaster from London, and they now set up a 'Revolutionary Policy Committee'. It argued for a sympathetic relationship with the Communist International, the reorganisation of the party on industrial lines, the formation of workers' councils, and the recognition of revolutionary methods of struggle. The ILP accepted the proposal for a united front with the CP on 17th March 1933 and its annual conference carried a resolution by 83 votes to 79 (against the recommendation of its National Administrative Council) instructing it to 'ascertain by what way the ILP may assist

in the work of the Communist International'. They began
negotiations with Manuilsky and Kuusinen in Moscow. For the time
being neither the leaders of the ILP nor Gaster and Cullen's
'Revolutionary Policy Committee' had much time for the British
Communist Party with its minute following and its repellent
sectarianism. But they do seem to have entertained illusions about
the way that this policy had been arrived at, giving Moscow the
benefit of the doubt and putting its excesses down to the
Comintern's British Section. They were soon to learn otherwise.
The reply of the Comintern was to suggest extending co-operation
with the CPGB to form 'a single, strong, mass Communist Party',
to ask the ILP to attack 'ruthlessly' the reformist Labour leaders, to
demand adherence to the suicidal 'United Front from Below', and to
reserve the right of criticism to the side of the Communist
International alone.

It was, in effect, a demand to liquidate their party and join with the
Communists on the basis of unconditional submission to the dictates
of the Executive of the Comintern, and both the ILP leaders and the
CPGB understood it as such. Pollitt himself boasted openly at a
public debate with C. A. Smith in Nottinghamshire that 'within a
year the CP and CI will win the majority of the ILP'.[17] For all the
Communists' protestations of 'unity', their manoeuvres were all too
plainly an attempt, not at agreement, but at a poaching expedition
among the ILP rank and file.

The ILP leaders were not impressed with this. Still less were they
impressed by the lofty dictation of the Comintern; and their
enthusiasm for its policies cooled when they saw the USSR expand
its trade with Nazi Germany at the time Communists abroad were
trying to get trade unions to black ships trading there. And more
precise information was coming in on how the Comintern treated its
sections. Brockway had met Jay Lovestone in America, in whose
purge from his majority position in the American CP Harry Pollitt
had played a not inconspicuous role. C. A. Smith had visited
Trotsky in France and come back with an enthusiastic account.[18] The
pages of the *New Leader* were thrown open to the contributions of
Lovestone, Trotsky and other dissident socialists and Communists.
The ILP published Trotsky's Copenhagen speech as a pamphlet with
a preface by Jimmy Maxton.[19] This free debate, in which Manuilsky
refused to take part[20] had the desired effect: the following York
Conference of the ILP at Easter 1934 rejected Gaster and Cullen's
proposal for 'conditional and sympathetic affiliation' to the Comintern by 98 votes to 51, and even day-to-day co-operation came to an
end.[21] For it had provoked a revolt in the ILP ranks; letters of
complaint deluged the national office, and a referendum showed that

two thirds of the members were uneasy or unwilling about the 'united front'. The South Wales area was taking part under protest. The Lancashire area broke off from the party in disgust. It was agreed on all sides that association with the Communists was impeding real and meaningful co-operation with the Labour Party, trades unions and co-ops, who would not touch the Communist Party with a barge pole.[22]

In the end, the impact of the Communists upon the ILP was less than expected. Despite Brockway's appeal that the Communists were using the ILP Guild of Youth 'to strike a blow at the ILP', it decided on sympathetic affiliation to the Young Communist International in May 1934,[23] only to reverse its decision at a special conference at Derby on November 18th.[24] After the defeat of the Communist faction—for that is what the Revolutionary Policy Committee had now become—at the 1935 conference, a large number of ILP youth resigned and announced their adherence to the YCL in the Moscow press.[25] As for the 'Revolutionary Policy Committee', they were, as the *Daily Worker* said, 'outmanoeuvred' by Brockway and Maxton[26] and by the time they also resigned, allegedly over the refusal of the ILP to withdraw the candidates it put up against the Labour Party in the general election, there were only some fifty of them left.[27]

It cannot be said that the British Communists had much success in the Unity Campaign. The inconsistencies of their propaganda were all too obvious. Before the turn was made the ILP was denounced as the 'left string' of Social Fascism, advanced by the Labour Party 'in order to influence the workers' whilst it moved 'more quickly than ever along the Social-Fascist path',[28] and Pollitt was telling Brockway that 'the ILP and the CP had nothing in common. It is war to the death'.[29] The communists had expelled Maxton from the British Section of the League Against Imperialism,[30] put up Saklatvala in an attempt to get McGovern defeated in the Shettleston by-election,[31] and made a formal decision in their Scottish District Secretariat to 'concentrate on constituencies occupied by 'lefts' like Maxton, Stephen and Kirkwood'.[32] Their handling of the Revolutionary Policy Committee had not been more subtle. 'There can be no united front with people who talk about 'revolutionary policy' but sabotage the fight against the capitalists and their lackeys, the Labour leaders' the *Daily Worker* declared in an attack upon Cullen.[33] The Revolutionary Policy Committee as a whole was described as 'in no degree in advance of Maxton-Brockway'[34] 'not concerned with fighting against the anti-working class policy of Brockway and co.',[35] and even (J. R. Campbell's gem, this) 'permeated with the counter-revolutionary nonsense of Trotsky'.[36]

Small wonder that Gaster was stung to criticise the CP for its 'narrow sectarianism', 'false approach' and 'virulent misrepresentation'.[37] It is all the more amazing that the RPC joined up with the Communists at all, a fact only explicable by the disintegration of the ILP and their lack of anywhere else to go. Even then Gaster hesitated a while before joining,[38] though he remains, a loyal member, to this day.

The change of line had been accomplished in a clumsy manner, in the full view of the rest of the Labour movement. The unexpected development of Communist Party policy had kept the leaders in the dark about the next steps, and they had been caught in more than one compromising position. Those who had condemned the Social Democrats for maintaining that 'the workers' movement must adapt itself to the petty bourgeoisie, must drop the narrow working-class basis, broaden its basis, take on a "national" character, etc'[39] were now advocating blocs, not only with the petty, but the big bourgeoisie, and embarrassing the labour movement with their anxiety to take on a 'national' colouration.[40] Those who had explained that 'an organisational compact with the Social Democrats means the liquidation of the revolutionary struggle',[41] and had called for 'no more coquetting with the "Left" leaders'[42] were now proposing marriage itself to 'democratic' (capitalist) politicians, and standing in defence of (bourgeois) democracy; and those who as late as February 1935 had prophesied that 'any Labour government' would mean 'the tying of the workers to capitalism'[43] were now supporting its election and doing their level best to do just that. It was a most unedifying spectacle of the ability of large numbers of serious people to turn about at the drop of a hat and advocate what they had hitherto been denouncing. And it was to get worse.

Footnotes

1 Resolution of the Central Committee of the KPD on the Situation and the Immediate Tasks, in *Inprecor*, vol. xiii, no. 24, 2nd June 1933, p. 525.
2 E. Varga, 'Results and Prospects of the German Fascism Now in Power', in *Inprecor*, vol. xiii, no. 27, 21st June 1933, p. 585.
3 *Immediate Tasks Before the Party and the Working Class*, CPGB pamphlet, 1932, p. 5.
4 *Daily Worker*, 8th March 1933.
5 *Daily Worker*, 11 March 1933.
6 TUC *Report* 1933, p. 174.

7 Allen Hutt, *The Post-War History of the British Working Class*, London, 1937, p 266.
8 *AEU Monthly* Journal, September, 1934.
9 Degras, *op.cit.*, vol. iii, p. 375.
10 W. Gallacher, *Pensioners of Capitalism*, CPGB Pamphlet, 1934, p. 14.
11 R. F. Andrews (Andrew Rothstein), *The Truth About Trotsky*, CPGB Pamphlet, February 1934, pp. 58-9.
12 *Rundschau* (German version of *Inprecor*), 8th March 1934, p. 712.
13 R. F. Andrews, 'Trotsky on Germany', in *Communist Review*, vol. v, no. 5, May 1933, P. 228.
14 R. F. Andrews, *The Truth About Trotsky*, CPGB Pamphlet, February 1934, p. 62.
15 W. Gallacher, *Pensioners of Capitalism*, CPGB Pamphlet, 1934, p. 30.
16 Fenner Brockway, *Inside the Left*, London 1942, pp. 239-40.
17 'The ILP and the CP', in the the *New Leader*, vol. xxiii, New Series, no. 70, 5th May 1933, p. 13.
18 'An Interview by C. A. Smith', in the *New Leader*, 13th October, 1933, cf. Vitte (Demetrius Giotopoulos), 'Report (to the International Secretariat) on the Situation of the English Section', Paris, 22nd September 1933; Interview with Brockway: 'I wanted you to know that in our organisation there is shown a great sympathy for the ideas of Comrade Trotsky', he told us. To the question posed, whether this sympathy shows itself in the active base of the organisation, he replied, 'I can assure you that what I think, also Maxton, Paton, Smith, think, and the same is proved by the organisation in London, to the measure that it can be proved'.
19 *Cf. The Early Years of the British Left Opposition: Five Previously Unpublished Letters by Leon Trotsky and Two Articles by Frank Ridley and James Maxton*, London, January 1979.
20 Fenner Brockway, 'The ILP and Moscow', in the *New Leader*, vol. xxiv, New Series, no. 106, 12th January 1934, p. 4.
21 'The ILP Conference', in the *New Leader*, vol. xxv, New Series, no. 12, 6th April 1934, p. 5.
22 Fenner Brockway, *Inside the Left*, London, 1942, pp. 252-3.
23 'Young Socialists Debate Policy', in the *New Leader*, vol. xxv, New Series, no. 19, 25th May 1934, p. 4.
24 'Young Socialists and the Communist International', in the *New Leader*, vol. xxvii, New Series, no. 43, 9th November, 1934.
25 *New Leader*, 28th June 1935; *Daily Worker*, 20th June 1935.
26 *Daily Worker*, 12th February 1934.
27 *Inprecor*, xv 1457f; 'Goodbye', the *New Leader*, vol. xxix, New Series, no. 55, 8th November 1935, p. 4.
28 William Rust, 'The Opposition in the ILP', in *Labour Monthly*, vol. xiii, no. 13, December 1931, p. 748.
29 *Daily Worker*, 29th April 1932; cf. below: 'unity with the ILP would be tantamount to a betrayal of the whole British working class'.
30 'Maxton Expulsion Supported', in the *Daily Worker*, 22nd May 1930.
31 *Daily Worker*, 28th June 1930.
32 *Daily Worker*, 5th July 1930.
33 'ILP Revolutionary Who Dares not Fight Leaders', in the *Daily Worker*, 11th April 1932.
34 R. Palme Dutt, 'Notes of the Month', in the *Labour Monthly*, vol. xiv, no. 8, August 1932, p. 481.
35 *Daily Worker*, 31st March 1932.
36 J. R. Campbell, 'Mr. Trotsky and the ILP', in *Communist Review*, vol. vi, no. 12,

December/January 1933/4, p. 435. *Cf* Rust's speech to the XIIIth Plenum of the ECCI, *Inprecor*, vol. xiv, no. 15, 5th March 1934, p. 381.

37 Jack Gaster, 'The Present Position of the ILP', in *Labour Monthly*, vol. 15, no. 1, January 1933.

38 'Goodbye!' in the *New Leader*, vol. xxix, New Series, no. 55, 8th November 1935, p. 4.

39 R. Palme Dutt, in *Labour Monthly*, October 1933, *cf.* the same writer's 'Notes of the Month', in *Labour Monthly*, vol. xx, no. 6, June 1938, p. 336.

40 *Cf.* below, pp 51-52.

41 W. Gallacher, 'We Have no Room for Trotskyists', in the *Daily Worker*, 23rd August 1932; *cf.* the same writer in *Labour Monthly*, vol. xviii, no. 2, February, 1936.

42 Tom Bell, 'The Crisis in our Party and the Way Out', in the *Communist Review*, vol. i, no. 12, December, 1929, p. 648.

43 R. Palme Dutt, in *Labour Monthly*, vol. xvii, no. 2, February 1935. *Cf.* the references in note 34 above.

Chapter Three

Showing the Flag, 1936-9

The late thirties provided an ideal setting for the turn of the Communists to Popular Front politics. The liberal conscience had received a shock at the coming to power of Hitler and the lack of resistance to Nazism from the traditional democratic parties. Persons of scientific inclination or cultural refinement were alarmed at the holocaust of German civilisation in the Wagnerian rituals of the Third Reich. Humanitarians everywhere were revolted at the treatment of the Jews, by the Nuremburg Laws and the Crystal Night. At home a complacent government presided over the sufferings of over a million unemployed. Abroad it temporised, or aided Hitler in his expansion, hoping that he might turn against the Soviet Union. Those who surveyed foreign affairs could not but contrast the stagnation of the capitalist economy with the expansion of Russian industry, or fail to understand the mortal hostility that existed between the USSR and Hitler's Germany. All these combined to create a favourable climate of opinion for the Communist Party, not only among workers but amongst traditional supporters of liberal democracy and even establishment figures. It was the great age of the 'fellow traveller'.

In itself, it was the embryo of a very positive development. The working class cannot come to power unless it draws in behind it other support, including sections of the middle and professional classes and the intelligentsia. The tragedy of the period was that there was no attempt to bring them round to a realisation of the necessity of working class revolution, the ideas of Marxism. Their illusions in capitalist democracy were fostered and their patriotism was kept intact. When most of them came round to denouncing Marxism as 'the God that failed' during the Cold War, there was little to show that they had ever tried the genuine article.

The motives of establishment figures who supported the Popular Front were cruder. They saw another opportunity to tie the working class parties to the capitalist state, and ultimately to provide support for imperialist war. A little cheer leading on behalf of Soviet Russia into the bargain was no more bad taste than previous remarks about gallant little Belgium, or brave France. Germany was going to be a tough nut to crack, and one more super power in the alliance was all to the better. In the meantime a Communist Party preaching the values of patriotism and democracy to the Labour Party was rather a useful thing to have.

Crucial for attracting the intellectuals were such literary ventures as *Left Review* and the Left Book Club. Behind a façade of broad left interest the Party pursued its narrow and particular aims. The Left Book Club, whose foundation in May 1936 brought the party a propaganda outlet with an ultimate audience of 57,000 maintained the pretence of a broad spectrum of writing to the right of and including the Communists (who contributed a third of the choices) whilst discriminating narrowly against the Left. Orwell's *Road to Wigan Pier* appeared with a patronising and insulting preface; *Homage to Catalonia* was outside the pale; and manuscripts by Thalheimer[1] and others critical of the CP line were rejected. Even advertisements for Trotsky's books were refused, for as Gollancz expressed it, 'a Trotskyist book falls as obviously outside the scope of the Club's publications as does a Nazi or a Fascist book'.[2] When suspicions were aroused that the Club was just a screen for the peculiar and particular preoccupations of the Communists, adjustments had to be made to maintain credibility. Gollancz wrote to Strachey on July 12th, 1937, saying that the question was 'a purely tactical one; our whole aim must be to win the maximum number of members and frighten the minimum'. 'In this connection', he added, 'Laski has suggested that we might get Attlee to do a general book on Labour policy. I am inclined to think that as a tactical move (accompanied by a suitable review in the *News*) it might be very useful'. (Hugh Thomas, *John Strachey*, London, 1963, p. 157.) The book they commissioned, Attlee's *The Labour Party in Perspective*, was quite critical of the Popular Front, and duly appeared along with instructions to convenors of local groups to contrast with it works that reflected the normal CP Line.[3]

That line was itself represented by large scale works of impudent lying, such as Dudley Collard's *Soviet Justice and the Trial of Radek and Others* and J. R. Campbell's *Soviet Policy and Its Critics*. So pronounced was the bias of the club that the Labour Party's National Agent was obliged to write to local constituency parties in March 1939 advising them not to join local groups, 'especially when these are in the direction of a so-called "Popular Front" with any other political party'.

It cannot be said that the Communist Party used the intellectual talent of its recruits and allies to develop Marxism in a constructive direction. Strachey, who shared with Gollancz and Laski the selection of Left Book titles, whom the Communist Party had hitherto dismissed as 'a young intellectual of a particularly unstable type'[4], was put up to exercise his not inconsiderable ability in analyses of 'Trotskyism'.[5] The influence of this mysterious entity was discerned in the pacifism of the ILP leaders and even the mainstream Labour opinion of the *Daily Herald*. A rigid orthodoxy was imposed on all. Stephen Spender himself had to write a public self-criticism when he joined the party after expressing some mild doubts about the Moscow Trials.[6] The truth was that these well-known figures received no Marxist training inside the party's ranks, except in the ephemera of the current 'line'. Instead, they were utilised in front scenarios or fund-raising appeals, or to lend credence to the peculiar venom with which the Communists pursued their opponents inside the labour movement, particularly on the Left.

Adulation of Stalin and utopian nonsense about the Soviet Union provided the Communists with a powerful advertising appeal, especially when it came out in vast and detailed statistics under the pens of well-known figures. The most extensive (and fatuous) of these was the Webbs' *Soviet Communism, a New Civilisation*, first appearing in 1935; the later edition even contained the Stalin Constitution, 'the most democratic in the world', whose chief author, Bukharin, was shortly to be a victim of the purges. It is remarkable that the authors should have taken seriously the mass of tendentious data provided for them, from such as had once damned them as 'openly saving capitalism at the workers' expense'[7], who were now no less enthusiastic in their praise.[8] But the Webbs were a classic example of how Communism attracted fellow travellers by appealing to ideas that they made no attempt to change. The Webbs' vision of socialism was of bureaucratic nationalisation and municipal control, which under no circumstances was ever to come under active administration by workers. The same instinct that had led them to condemn the Russia of Lenin now attracted them to the Stalinist state. It was not the case, as Trotsky maintained, that they failed to distinguish between the face of a revolution and its backside: they knew the difference well enough, but preferred the backside.

Of course the appeal of Communism in its most right wing phase was not intended to stop short at the Labour intelligentsia. Such MPs as Acland (N. Devon), Le Mander (Wolverhampton E.) and Roberts (Cumberland N.) and such respectable newspapers as the *Guardian* and the *News Chronicle* supported the Popular Front campaign. The Editor of the latter, A. J. Cummings, was so fervent in his support for the Moscow Trials[9] as to earn the praise of Harry Pollitt at the Communist Party's annual conference.[10] Pundits and commentators, vicars and scientists, poets and philosophers, dissident Liberals and high Tories, in brief, all such as disagreed with the policy of the National Government on 'patriotic' lines, were enlisted by the Communists in their drive against the independence of the labour movement.

Almost instinctively, leadership and rank and file moved to defend it. The position of Labour and trade union leaders in parliament and at a national level depended upon the solid bloc of workers' support behind them; and the experiences of the twenties had taught substantial sectors of the working class how little they could rely upon establishment and liberal circles to protect them. Before January 1936 was out, Labour's secretary had written to Pollitt refusing the Communists' request for affiliation;[11] and this was followed by a salvo in July describing their motives as being 'for the purpose of subjecting the Labour and trade union movement of Great Britain to the dictation of the Russian government',[12] making the observation that 'the Communists are now active in practicing that class collaboration that they have so roundly denounced in the past'. When the time came to debate the issue at Labour Party Conference at Edinburgh in October 1936, neither the support of the most middle class section of the movement, the Fabian Society, nor of some of the local Labour parties and the smaller unions availed against the mass trade union votes, and affiliation was rejected over whelmingly. An amendment asking the National Executive to 'take all practicable steps to mobilise the support of all peace-loving and democratic citizens in the struggle for peace and the fight against Fascism' was even more ignominiously defeated. Worst of all for the Communists was the unanimous support accorded to a resolution 'irrevocably opposed to any attempt to "liberalise" the Labour Party by "watering down" its policy in order to increase its membership'.[13] The Communist case was not helped by importing into the debate such devices as the smear and the amalgam, such as when the mover of the first motion, A. H. Paton of Edinburgh Trades and Labour Council, asked if it was 'only an accident that the National Council (i.e. of Labour) should speak with the voice of Goebbels?'[14]

The strongest opponents of the Popular Front were the trade union leaders. Dallas opposed co-operation with the Liberals. Bevin later even threatened disaffiliation if the policy went through:

'Trades unions have confidence in their own political party, not in

other parties; and if by chance this situation be changed, many
trade unions would revert to freedom of action and would not
acknowledge any obligation to any "Popular" Party that might
be formed.'[15]

As far as Dalton was concerned, the proposals were 'clotted
nonsense'. Attlee put his finger on the question when he wrote:

> 'The plain fact is that a Socialist Party cannot hope to make a
> success of administering the capitalist system because it does not
> believe in it. That is a fundamental objection to all the proposals
> that are put forward for the formation of a Popular Front in this
> country.'[16]

When Elvin, Chairman of the TUC that year, spoke for the
independence of Labour, he earned the following reply from Willie
Gallacher:

> 'Take Mr. Elvin on the Popular Front. "It means the sacrifice of
> our independence", he declares, "it means associating with the
> capitalists. This we cannot do. We must keep our Socialist
> principles pure." I don't think it would be possible to get more
> cynical demagogy than this.
>   For if there is one thing obvious above all others, it is that Mr.
> Elvin and the General Council (i.e. of the TUC) are prepared not
> only to associate with the big capitalists but with the National
> Government of the big capitalists.'[17]

As far as the Labour leadership went this might have been
demagogy, but support for the unity of Labour against its enemies
was carried by the *Daily Herald* into the ranks, stirring up feelings of
class-consciousness. For reason supported elemental feeling. Take
the following letter from an assistant secretary of a Labour Party in
the provinces:

> '(It is) impossible to work with Liberals, they are a capitalist
> party. The results of the Popular Front in Spain and France have
> been calamitous to the working-class movement in those
> countries. In Spain in spite of the superhuman efforts of the
> Government forces the Government has been brought to its
> knees. They are fighting for an abstract idea, "capitalist
> democracy", which does not exist.'[18]

The opening of the great purge trials with the process of the

Sixteen in August 1936, accompanied by the murder of incalculable numbers of lesser folk, was another policy of the Soviet Union that had international repercussions. Its main intention had been to complete the despotic structure that Stalin had built over the grave of the Russian Revolution. It was the final, crowning step, in the Stalinisation of the state apparatus. But as in all countries where the state monopolises the media, these great trials were meant to play a propaganda role, not the least in foreign policy. Foreigners could hardly miss the point that here on trial were all that remained of the great revolutionaries of 1917, or that foreign Communists within Russia supplied a disproportionate share of the victims. They were a grisly reminder that Soviet Russia had really abandoned the world revolution, that it really did stand for the defence of 'democracy' through the Popular Front. The bodies of Kun, Remmele and Neumann proved it, as did the accusations of plotting with Germany made throughout the trials. The victims of Stalin's Russian despotism were also human sacrifices on the altar of the Popular Front. The extension of the terror to Spain made the point all too clearly.

This was certainly meant to be the message for the bourgeois supporters of the People's Front in Britain. As R. Page Arnot confidently affirmed,

'The answer of all those outside the ranks of the working class, who have rallied to the defence of democracy in Spain, must be to deepen and extend that democratic front of support to democracy, and to use the Moscow Trial as one of the best examples of how a real democracy can defend itself against fascism.'[19]

The stand of the Labour and Socialist International, the Second International (to which was affiliated the British Labour Party) was a thousand miles to the left of any of the Communist parties on this question, who vied with Vyshinsky himself in their denunciations of the accused. Adler wrote a pamphlet exposing the inconsistencies of the trial. Dalton and Dallas, as representatives of British Labour on the Executive of the International, supported him. Citrine signed the official appeal of de Brouckère (President) and Adler (Secretary) on behalf of the International in his capacity as representing the International Federation of Trades Unions. The appeal regretted the trial being held, asked for a defence council for the victims independent of the government, and requested that the death sentence be not used. Citrine's reward for this was to be accused of

siding 'with traitors',[20]and when the *Daily Herald* published an
interview with Adler, they were asked to make the link between his
'active support of criminals in the USSR' and 'the persistent refusal
of the Labour and Socialist International to act in face of danger to
democracy'[21] (i.e. support the Popular Front as a whole). For its
exposure of the falsity of the trials the *Daily Herald* was lectured by
Labour fellow-travellers of the CP for playing 'the game of
reaction',[22] defending 'spies and assassins',[23] and 'foul lies'.[24] In
particular, its suggestion that the death of Ordzhonikidze might not
have been entirely a natural one earned it the title of 'the most
scurrilous rag in the newspaper world',[25] 'whose columns seemed
always open to reflect the identical desires of the Trotskyists and of
the German embassy'.[26]

The Labour leaders would have been less than human if they had
not followed the lead of the Communists in linking together the
trials and the Popular Front, and used it as excellent propaganda
material to discredit the 'unity' campaign. Over and over again the
CP damned the *Herald* 'with contempt' for stooping 'so low as to say
that the Moscow Trial shows that the affiliation of the Communist
Party to the Labour Party should not now be accepted'.[27] At the same
time a meeting of the Parliamentary Labour Party went on record
deploring the Trials, and the ILP MPs joined Brockway in
addressing an official appeal to Stalin. Disbelief combined with
suspicion of the Popular Front in the minds of Labour activists, in
sharp contrast to the howl of approval from the cultured and learned
allies of the Communist Party. As Laski noted:

> 'There is no doubt the mass executions in the Soviet Union in the
> last two years have greatly injured the prestige of Russia with the
> rank and file of the Labour Party. They do not understand them,
> and they feel that those who accept them without discussion are
> not satisfactory allies. I do not comment on this view; I merely
> record it. In my judgement, the executions undoubtedly cost the
> supports of the United Front (sic!) something like half a million
> votes at the Bournemouth Conference.'

It was a thought which struck Fenner Brockway at the same time:

> 'I took the trouble to make enquiries in all parts of the country to
> discover the reasons for the setback which the cause of unity had
> received at various trade union conferences—the most striking
> instance was that of the miners, who the previous year had
> supported unity and this year rejected it—and I was surprised to
> find how general was the explanation, that the series of executions

in Russia had turned the workers against association with the Communist Party. This reaction had gone wide and deep into the ranks of the working classes.'[28]

The executions made an impact upon Laski as well as Brockway. From being a supporter of the CP 'unity' campaign he moved gradually over to complete rejection, and was co-author with Dalton, Greenwood and Morrison of the NEC's reply to the 'unity' proposals in *Labour and the Popular Front*.[29] He remained a determined and articulate enemy of the Communists throughout the wartime and post-war periods, when so many of the other fellow-travellers had their second honeymoon with the Soviet Union.

Rejected in their frontal approach, the Communist Party next tried to float a Popular Front by a more roundabout route. They approached the ILP (again) and the Socialist League with proposals for a 'Unity Campaign' involving themselves to begin with, then directed to the Labour Party, then hopefully (in the CP's estimation at least) towards an alliance with 'Progressives' outside the Labour movement. It was neither an easy nor a straightforward strategy—failure in any of the stages would doom the whole project, and its internal weaknesses were obvious. The ILP had already had quite enough of the CP's unity manoeuvres, and a legacy of distrust remained, especially among the rank and file. The problem of the right of criticism for the ILP parliamentary group also remained, the original cause of the split from the Labour Party, on which the Labour Party itself remained adamant.

There were difficulties even with the Socialist League. This body, founded in October 1932 at a conference in Leicester, consisted of all those ex-members of the ILP who had disagreed with the split with the Labour Party, and remained inside it. The League was affiliated to the Labour Party, as the old ILP had been, and enjoyed the patronage, if not the wholehearted support, of influential Labour Party figures. George Lansbury attended its founding conference, and it was supported by a number of MPs, such as Aneurin Bevan and George Strauss. Its membership, estimated at some 3,000, was largely middle class, and its secretary was J. T. Murphy, expelled from the Communist Party in March 1932 over the confused and trivial issue of whether the Party should support credits for expanding trade with the Soviet Union. Its National Chairman after November 1933 was a wealthy lawyer, Sir Stafford Cripps, who had hesitated before joining, when he moved rapidly over to a left wing position as enthusiastic as it was naive.

The relations of the Socialist League with the Communist Party in the past had been none too smooth. Attacks upon the Socialist

League were mounted in the *Daily Worker* as soon as it had been launched,[30] and for years afterwards Cripps and the others were being dismissed as 'chatterers',[31] and the Socialist League itself as trying 'to provide a screen for the reactionary policy of the Labour Party'.[32] When the Communist Party switched its policy from the Third Period to the Popular Front the political differences had widened rather than narrowed, with the Socialist League occupying a position on the political spectrum well to the left of the Communists. The MPs, Strauss and Bevan, it is true, were Popular Fronters throughout, and J. T. Murphy remained an unrepentant Stalinist to his death, albeit without a party card, as his memoirs show. But Cripps swore he would never support a Popular Front, and led the opposition to unity with the CP at the League's annual conference in 1935. The League as a whole disagreed with CP reliance on the 'collective security' of the League of Nations, and particularly on the policy of sanctions, which they regarded as leading inevitably to imperialist war, and carried out a determined struggle against it at the Labour Party Conference of October 1935.

When the Abyssinian crisis began the Socialist League called mass meetings all over the country to protest at the threat to peace from Mussolini, and to win support for their policy of opposition to imperialist war. Their conference in London was attended by over 1,500 delegates from various labour movement bodies. The main opposition to the Socialist League came from those under Communist influence, who supported the sanctions policy of the League of Nations. For Soviet Russia had just joined the League of Nations for the first time. At this Murphy, who had written the Socialist League's pamphlet on Fascism, and had been proud to announce to the Communists that the League had now changed its policy and supported their affiliation to the Labour Party[33] resigned his membership.

The Socialist League moved steadily leftwards. Its annual conference at Whitsun 1936 reaffirmed its opposition to the League of Nations and to the policies of 'Peace Fronts' and Popular Fronts against a long list of Communist resolutions and amendments trying to support them. Feeling the need for allies abroad, it agreed to send an observer to the meetings of the International Bureau for Revolutionary Socialist Unity, a group of Socialist Parties including the British ILP which stood to the left of the Communist International.

Another source of irritation for the Communist Party was the small but vocal group of Trotskyists who began to play an influential rôle in the League. Denzil Harber was organiser of the sales of the League's paper in London for a while,[34] and Reg Groves had been elected onto its executive in September 1935,[35] as well as being Chairman of its London Area Commmittee, and writing several of its pamphlets and lecturing widely for it. Articles by himself and Jack Winnocour appearing regularly in the League's press followed the dismal track record of the Popular Front abroad[36], and encouraged disquiet among the rank and file with both the Moscow Trials and the policy of the Communists in the Spanish Civil War. The League even officially supported the call of the International Bureau for an independent investigation into the purges. It was plain that the Socialist League would be no easy ally for the Communists, and was fast becoming an embarrassment. Even Cripps himself had an ultra-left past not unlike the Communists' 'Third Period', when he had analysed the National Government as 'fascist',[37] and to the annoyance of all sorts of reformists had denied that Socialism could be attained by purely constitutional methods.[38]

The Communists had to maintain a measure of circumspection (to say the least), and they initiated secret negotiations with Cripps, Mellor and some of the MPs without notifying the League's membership. Pollitt and Dutt had been treating with Cripps in his chambers for some months before the League even heard about it in November 1936. When the National Council were let in on the secret they also were sworn to silence, as very delicate negotiations were still going on. Groves was the only member of the League's council to object to the Unity Campaign in itself, though a few others objected to the terms on which it was offered. But Cripps had done a complete turn round. 'Cripps jettisoned the policy of the Socialist League', wrote Groves many years later, 'as in his legal practice, he passed from one brief to another, from a brief for revolutionary Socialism to a new brief for the united front, without any noticeable difficulty. But it was not just the interests of clients involved here—but principles and policies affecting many people.' (Reg Groves, *A Documentary History of the Socialist League*, unpublished Ms., p. 16.) Feeling that it was unprincipled for the leading body to carry on in this way behind the backs of the membership, he took it upon himself to send a circular round the branches. Realising the political dynamite it contained, someone sent a copy to the *Daily Herald*, which promptly spilled the beans. Despite his protest to the contrary,[39] the *Daily Worker* accused him of sending it to Transport House and to the Herald, and of attacking the Unity Campaign through its pages.[40]

In the meantime, other difficulties had arisen on the negotiating committee, where the League was represented by Mellor and Cripps, the CP by Pollitt and Dutt, and the ILP by Brockway and Maxton. Negotiations broke down six times. The ILP delegates refused to endorse the concept of the Popular Front on which the CP insisted, and a way out of the deadlock was only found by referring it to the Socialist League and the Communists for revision. Back it came again, with the offending concept in the alternative form of 'for the defence of the Soviet Union and its fight for peace, and for a pact between Great Britain, the Soviet Union, France and all other states in which the working class have political freedom'. The ILP simply did not believe that Russia was contributing to peace by entering imperialist alliance systems, and sought to replace the last clause (itself a compromise suggested by the Socialist League) with a pact between working class governments. In the end, the ILP signed, whilst expressing their dissent on these points in a memorandum addressed to Cripps personally. When the ILP published it, Dutt and Pollitt (under no such obligations to their own supporters) were beside themselves with fury.

The policy had still to be sold to the Socialist League. Pollitt had gradually gained ascendancy over Cripps, though Mellor was in opposition to the Popular Front from a Marxist standpoint. The confusion of the other League members was reflected by the vote at the special delegate conference which met to consider the matter on January 16th-17th 1937, ratifying the agreement by 56 votes, as against 38 and 23 abstentions. Groves and other oppositionists had a shrewd suspicion that the CP wanted to destroy the League, for Transport House could hardly be congenial to one of its organisations being used as a Trojan horse for a policy so firmly rejected by annual conference.

No long time was to pass before their fears were justified.

The Unity Campaign was launched at a public meeting addressed by Pollitt, Cripps and Maxton on January 24th, 1937, at the Free Trade Halls in Manchester. This was appropriate enough, as nothing symbolised traditional Liberalism quite so much as free trade, though the subtle irony of this seemed to escape them. But the NEC of the Labour Party was far from Liberal, for they promptly disaffiliated the Socialist League three days later by a vote of 23 to 9. And to show they really meant it, a further decision on the 24th March declared that after 1st June membership of the Socialist League and of the Labour Party were to be incompatible.

The League met to consider the threat at a special conference held in Leicester on May 16th. The alternatives were quite clear—to withdraw from the Unity Campaign, or be expelled from the Labour Party. A report published in the co-operative paper *Reynolds News* showed that Labour leaders were considering drastic action against the supporters of the Unity Campaign.[41] Pollitt suggested that the League should go into voluntary dissolution to free its members to campaign for unity within the Labour Party, which was immediately seized on by Cripps (who had just written a policy document arguing the necessity for the Socialist League!). Mellor stuck to this view, arguing that otherwise they would play into the hands of the right wing leadership in Transport House, who wanted to be rid of the League as a separately organised Left formation. He was supported by Groves, who urged that the League should continue to exist, whilst pointing out that those who supported the Unity Campaign would still be left free to support it as individuals. They gained a mere 10 votes, as against Cripps' 57, and the Socialist League declared itself to be in suspension until the Labour Conference in October would afford the opportunity to reverse the decision. The next blow fell when the NEC meeting on May 25th-26th condemned the decision of the disbanded League to continue the campaign for 'unity', and denounced the whole thing in a document addressed to its organisations.[42]

The Annual Conference met at Bournemouth in October 1937. A resolution was put down to support the Popular Front, and Cripps, Laski and Strauss tried to refer back the NEC report, *The Socialist League and Party Loyalty*.[43] Herbert Morrison in particular drew upon the resources of his Marxist training as an ex-member of the Social Democratic Federation to mount a devastating attack upon the whole idea of a Popular Front:

'Suppose that Mr. Trotsky came to London, and it was suggested by the ILP that there should be a United Front meeting with Jimmie Maxton, Harry Pollitt, and Leon Trotsky as principal speakers. Mr. Trotsky is a Socialist. He was the chairman of the Military Revolutionary Committee which had a great deal to do with the Bolshevist Revolution in Russia. I myself, if I had to choose between Mr. Stalin, as a practical hard-headed administrator, and Mr. Trotsky, whom I am bound to agree I think is a bit up in the air, temperamentally then, as an administrator myself, I would be inclined to sympathise with Stalin rather than Trotsky. But Trotsky is a Socialist. Would Mr. Pollitt appear on a platform with Socialist, working-class Trotsky? He would not. If some of the leaders of the POUM in Spain, a working-class party, came to London, and the ILP wanted another United Front platform with them and Mr. Pollitt, Mr. Pollitt would not appear. But Mr. Pollitt will appear with the Duchess of Atholl.'[44]

In the laughter that followed, there was little more to be said. The 'united' front was rejected by 2,116,000 votes to 331,000, and the reference back of the report on the Socialist League by 1,730,000 to

373,000. The Socialist League was never revived, though Groves and other opponents of the idea of dissolution tried to keep it alive under the label of the 'Socialist Left Federation'. Their one-sided struggle to keep Labour's only left ginger group earned for them the accusation of 'pursuing their usual wrecking tactics' from the CP.[45]

The real wreckers were the Communists themselves, who had urged this impossible course for the League in the first place. Groves and the others had forecast that very result. In later years Brockway began to ponder the question as to whether the Communists did it deliberately.[46] Evidence accumulated since suggests that this is so,[47] for the next phase of the CP policy was to organise their own entry work within the Labour Party on a vast scale, to secure the direct affiliation of their own party. Support for the 'Unity Campaign' by the ex-members of the Socialist League on an individual basis could only take the form of assisting this campaign. At the same time a possible left rival was liquidated in whose ranks considerable disquiet had been growing about the Popular Front's poor showing abroad and the butchery of the Moscow Trials.

Harsh as it seemed, Labour's verdict on Cripps and his friends was well-founded. It can be substantiated by a simple analysis of the evolution of *Tribune*, a paper founded by Cripps in January 1937. Mellor, who opposed both the Popular Front, and the liquidation of the League, had to resign the editorship; it began to assume the familiar features of Stalinism, in its defence of the Moscow Trials, reproduction of Stalin's and other official Russian statements, support for the Communists' dubious activities in Spain, and Cripps' own advocacy of a full-blown and open Popular Front line.[48] It even commissioned Pat Sloan, the author of such fables as *Soviet Democracy* to do a demolition job upon Trotsky's *The Revolution Betrayed*, and Campbell's *Soviet Policy and its Critics* was praised to the skies.

The ship of the Unity Campaign was coming apart at the seams, foundering on the rocks of incompatibility. The day of the Popular Front was over. Labour activists were quite capable of drawing the political conclusions of its balance sheet abroad, as the following letter from L. H. Meakin to *Tribune* on April 22nd shows:

'Since then, Popular Front stock, which as Cripps admits has its basis in class collaboration, has scarcely been high. While Barcelona's militant leaders are suppressed as "Trotsky-Fascist agents", Franco carried all before him, and every effort of Blum to help Spain, and even to introduce that "Labour reformism" is resisted by the Senate and the reactionary elements it represents.

France, today, is nearer to a Fascist counter-attack than Britain, and every intelligent man must realise it.

Yet Cripps is convinced of the necessity for a Popular Front in Britain, of everybody to the Left of Chamberlain. How are the mighty fallen!'

Yet the leaders of the 'Unity Campaign', the British Popular Front, stuck to the letter of their agreement; even after the provocations mounted by the Stalinists in Spain against the ILP's sister party, the POUM, McNair could still explain to Dutt that 'the important thing to have in mind is that the Unity Campaign in Britain should engender unity in Spain rather than allow Spanish disunity to break up the Unity Campaign in Britain'.[49] But this 'unity' at that moment in Spain was outlawing the POUM and torturing its leader to death by tearing off his skin, and would hardly impress the rank and file of the ILP. They were asking pertinent questions about the value of 'unity' with the perpetrators of the Moscow Trials and 'flaming' with 'controversy'[50] against their CP brethren. But even when 'unity' broke down completely the leaders of both organisations were still trying to blame each other for the rift in this most unnatural marriage.[51]

The policy of the Popular Front had its own terrible logic, whatever the motives of those promoting it, and that was the destruction of the organisations of the working class. 'Thus ended ingloriously the Unity Campaign', observed Brockway. 'Its result was the destruction of the Socialist League, the loss of influence of Cripps, Bevan, Strauss and other "Lefts", the strengthening of the reactionary leaders, and the disillusionment of the rank and file.'[52] And, adds Dewar significantly, 'a further weakening of the moribund ILP to the benefit of the CPGB'.[53] Such were the bitter fruits of the second stage of the CP's campaign for the Popular Front.

The third phase of the campaign was to take the form of an attack, not only upon the independence of the Labour Party, but even on its very existence in the rural districts, a liquidation of the party outside its main centres for the benefit of Liberals and 'democratic' Tories. It was an attempt to return to the conditions of the 1880s. Having disposed of the Socialist League and the ILP, the Communists planned to do this by getting their allies in the Labour Party to agitate for affiliation again, supporting it by large scale entry or fraction work inside. With the expansion of Germany, leading to the Munich crisis and then on to the Second World War, everyone's attention was quite naturally focussed on foreign affairs. The Communists grew ever desperate to remove the National Government and replace it by no matter what means with a government of no matter what sort that would provide an ally for the Soviet Union. Given the conditions of the time their appeal could only be to patriotism, to those who felt that the Chamberlain government was not serving the real interests of the nation. It marked another step towards the right, for it appealed to Tories who were even more nationalist than the largely Conservative government. The world crisis was propelling the Popular Front policy towards its logical conclusion—an attack upon the labour movement by patriots, war mongers and 'democrats'—all, of course, in the cause of 'peace'.

Conditions existed for a more effective operation than before. A change in the rules of the Labour Party at the Bournemouth Conference had produced a different method of election to the NEC in the constituency section, and Cripps, Laski and Pritt, all supporters of 'unity' had been elected. Behind them the CP intensified its faction work. Already in November 1936 official sources were complaining that 'Communists have eaten far deeper into local Labour Parties than is realised'.[54] As the trades unions were more firm against the Popular Front, and in any case possessed a stronger structure, the CP decided to concentrate on the constituency parties. Even in the big towns these were often mere shells, for like any other electoral apparatus the Labour Party dwindles in activity and commitment when there are no elections taking place, and taking over rural districts and middle class suburban areas was the simplest task imaginable. Charlotte Haldane describes how she entered St. Pancras Borough Council as a Labour member whilst holding a Communist Party card, and how her husband continued in this position until he became openly identified with the CP in 1942.[55] Douglas Hyde gives an account of how he organised the infiltration and complete takeover of a divisional Labour Party in a 'backward' district in Surrey.[56] Any recruits to the CP from the Labour Party were kept inside, and some were directed in from outside to function as 'cryptos' for the Communist Party. So successful were they that over 120 constituency parties represented at a conference held to aid Spain in 1938 declared themselves in favour of the Popular Front.

But their greatest success was in the Labour League of Youth. It was a real tragedy, for unlike the Young Communist League, which was largely itself middle class, the Labour Party's youth section was almost entirely proletarian. Helped by professional organisers and large amounts of money, CP supporters led by Ted (later Lord) Willis around the paper *Advance* captured control of its National Administrative Council as early as the League of Youth Conference of 1936. It was used to assist their entrists in the adult party, as well as for promoting the full Popular Front line among young people. The LLOY found itself sponsoring such things as a rally held at Earl's Court to launch a 'Peace Bloc' along with the YCL, the University

Youth Federation, the Young Liberals and the League of Nations Youth. The 1938 Conference of the League even despatched a telegram of good wishes to the Duchess of Atholl, whilst the fraternal delegate from the London Labour Party was obliged to warn Willis and his friends about their current obsession with 'discussions on Trotskyism', 'as this is not an issue in the Labour Party'.[57] *Advance*, which was to become the League's official newspaper, was crammed with Stalinist propaganda justifying the Moscow Trials and the Spanish Popular Front, not only from Willis and his friends, but even from Dutt, Bert Papworth and John Gollan, secretary of the YCL, whose work was reviewed under the heading of *At Last: Someone Who Speaks for Youth*. Joint hikes were arranged with the YCL, and several League branches were represented at the latter's Bermondsey Conference. So obvious was this 'co-operation' that few in the adult party any longer paid any attention to anything that the Youth section had to say: a letter in the July 1939 *Advance* pointed out that 'if the League of Youth appeared as willing to work with the Labour Party as they are to work with the YCL and the Unity Campaign their Conference decisions would be taken more seriously'.

Mechanically, the Labour League of Youth began to follow the twists and turns of Moscow's politics. Willis went on to call for a war against Germany, and persuaded large numbers of League members to join the Territorials. Finally, in June 1939 he and his supporters pulled out to join the YCL, leaving the Labour League of Youth in ruins.[58] By this time hardly a week went by when the *Daily Worker* failed to carry a report that such and such officers, councillors or GMC delegates, Communist entrists, had resigned from the Labour Party to join the ranks of the CP.[59] The numbers of these and the fact that important figures such as Pritt and Haldane were kept in to do damage at some future date illustrates the scale of this fantastic operation.

It was carefully organised fraction work, not undertaken with the aim of promoting the unity of the labour movement, or of spreading revolutionary ideas inside it, but to bring pressure to bear on local Labour Parties not to split the anti-Tory vote by standing candidates in by-elections against Liberals and 'progressives', and to disrupt the party on a national scale in the interests of a multi-class bloc.

The NEC of the Labour Party understood this when (for the umpteenth time) they rejected the Popular Front proposals in April 1938. They issued a circular on the 12th reminding affiliates of the previous conference decision, appealing to them not to lose faith in the cause of Labour, ('definitely to plan for a Labour victory'), and declared 'against the weakening of party policy to accommodate other political elements'.

By this time the Communist Party was not so much diluting its own brew as watering down the water. In the May of 1938 it rechristened its campaign 'The United Peace Alliance', of 'democratic peoples of all political parties' who were 'working desperately to build *A PEACE ALLIANCE THAT WILL DEFEAT CHAMBERLAIN* and set up a People's Government pledged to join Britain to the democratic countries in a strong Peace Bloc which can stop war'.[60] Classes and parties were to dissolve in a great popular soup; and questions of class and government were to boil away into a sort of hot-pot treaty:

> 'The Peace Bloc means an alliance of peace-loving nations, all of which are pledged to help each other against aggression. It threatens no-one and is open to any nation which genuinely wishes to prevent war.'[61]

But no such alliance existed; no capitalist governments could be described as 'peace-loving', especially at the end of the thirties; and no international chef existed who could taste how 'genuine' were their desires for peace (unless, of course, the Communist Party had Stalin in mind).

The dish was appreciated in some quarters, for the Co-op, meeting in congress in Easter 1938, supported it by a vote of 2,343,000 to 1,947,000. The policy was tested in a by-election which came up at Aylesbury in May, 1938. As chance would have it, the candidate selected by the local party a year before was Reg Groves, who had led the fight against liquidation and the Unity Campaign inside the Socialist League. Party Headquarters were worried that Groves' well-known leftism would lose them votes, and assist the Communists' drive against Labour in the country areas, and invited him to discuss the matter with the National Agent at Transport House. They wanted him to stand down in favour of a less controversial candidate, a retired army colonel; but in the end they reluctantly agreed to leave it to the discretion of the local party.

The union and local party delegates met for the selection conference at Aylesbury Town Hall. Groves and the local delegates waited downstairs, whilst above the executive wrangled for hours with the representative of Transport House. There were a number of 'concealed' Communists on the executive (which consisted for the most part of those who had cars, to be able to get to meetings in the different parts of the constituency), and they argued first of all that Labour should withdraw to give the Liberals a free run against the government candidate. When this got them nowhere they switched to supporting the nominee favoured by Transport House, reasoning that if the colonel whom they had proposed secured the nomination, the local people would lose heart and concede the fight. At the same time the utmost pressure was brought to bear against the Aylesbury Party from outside. The Labour parliamentary candidate for Northampton, R. T. Paget, wrote to *Tribune* on the 6th May to suggest that a referendum be held through the Labour candidates association asking for the Aylesbury party to withdraw its nominees. The local party reacted angrily to this attempt to override their rights in a letter signed by R. Orchard, Secretary of the Buckinghamshire Federation of Trades Councils and Labour Parties, which came out in *Tribune's* next issue:

'Your correspondent, R. T. Paget suggests that a referendum of Labour candidates be taken to discover whether opinion in the movement favours supporting the Liberal candidate or fighting the seat at Aylesbury.

That is surely a matter for the comrades in Mid Bucks alone, and one would think with the lessons of history before us compromise on this matter would be the last thing we should think about. What happened to the Liberal Party after the coalition of 1916? Where is it now?

No, to throw the comrades of Mid Bucks to the wolves for the sake of a gesture to the Liberals is not, in my opinion, the way to power. Where is all our propaganda of past years about Liberals and Tories being capitalist parties tarred with the same brush? The evidence of every sort of compromise of this nature has always been that in the long run it does not pay.

Our friends of Mid Bucks had much better fight and keep the flag flying than combine to defeat Toryism and still find themselves on the losing side, thus giving Chamberlain the greater victory.

Our position in Mid Bucks has not been achieved without heroic effort against overwhelming obstacles. Compromise now and we are lost there as a party.

We shall not achieve a Socialist Commonwealth by compromise of this sort.'

Even the young Reg (now Lord) Underhill wrote in to support them in the following number of *Tribune*, pointing out that it was the desertion of the Liberal vote to the Tories in the 1935 election in Paget's own constituency that had cost Labour the seat! In any case, class lines and political commitment are often more firmly rooted in country areas, where no opportunities exist for those who join the

Labour Party for personal advancement. The slightest glance at conference resolutions from such constituencies even today shows a brave and militant spirit. The Aylesbury party refused to budge. As Groves recalls,

> 'They expected the local Labour Party people who had lived their years building a Labour Party, sticking up for the Labour Party against the Liberals, to go back on it. They wouldn't, of course, they wouldn't do it.'[62]

The Communists now got a number of prominent people whose rôle in the local party was limited to paying subscriptions, to leave and support the Liberal, Atholl Robertson, an old-fashioned free trader. They signed a manifesto along with Brailsford, Lord Addison and others backing his candidature; it circulated around the constituency whilst the *Daily Worker* denounced Groves as a 'friend of Chamberlain' and 'an agent of Franco'. As Dutt summarised it,

> '. . . the manoeuvres of Trotskyism, in association with Transport House have succeeded in creating disruption within the Divisional Labour Party . . . The issue of Socialism is not the issue of this election. There is no question of which of the candidates stands for the United Peace Alliance against Chamberlain and can defeat Chamberlain if unity is achieved. The fact that this candidate bears the Liberal label is secondary in the present critical issue to the fact that he stands for the unity of the democratic forces for peace against Chamberlain and fascism. We could have wished that agreement between the local working class and democratic organisations could have been achieved to support one candidate. The pressure of Transport House prevented this.
>
> The only course in Aylesbury is to give their votes for the candidate who stands for the United Peace Alliance and can defeat Chamberlain.'[63]

This was a most extraordinary crossing of class lines by those who had promoted the slogan of 'class against class' not so long before. As the ILP observed,

> 'At Aylesbury the Communist Party supported a candidate of a Capitalist Party against the candidate of the Working-class Party. Nothing can excuse or remove that betrayal.'[64]

But they did excuse it. Strachey revealed the thinking behind it using a logic that would restrict Labour to fighting inner city seats alone, and in effect giving up all hope of forming a government:

> 'The Peace Alliance would involve the withdrawal of Labour
> candidates from perhaps 50 "Aylesburys"; from 50 seats, that is to
> say, in which the Labour Party has not the faintest chance of
> victory: from 50 seats in which the real choice lies simply between
> a Chamberlain supporter and an anti-Chamberlain Liberal . . . Far
> more important, however, is the psychological consideration.
> The fact that Labour was willing to support non-Labour pro-
> gressives in seats of the Aylesbury type would unquestionably
> bring in enormous non-Labour support to candidates in just those
> seats which can only be won by Labour if the Labour candidates
> become the effective representatives of all the progressive forces
> in the area.'[65]

National attention was focussed on Aylesbury. Groves was not
intimidated, but fought the campaign on an old-fashioned class war
platform. When the result came in the Tory vote had dropped by
3,033, the Liberal by 2,871, and Labour's had risen by 3,000 on a
heavy poll, saving its deposit in the constituency for the first time. It
was a response to a class appeal: its message for the Communist Party
was no less obvious. In calling it 'one of the most brilliant Labour
achievements for a long while', the *Daily Herald* added 'if we were
"Popular Fronters" we would take a look at the Aylesbury result and
then crawl off home'.[66]

Whatever message there was, it was lost on the CP. Commenting
upon Groves' remark that 'the Peace Alliance has been completely
exposed', they could only record that 'there will be loud cheers at the
result in Transport House. The increase in the Labour vote will be
taken as justification for their opposition to the United Peace
Alliance . . . it was right to call Groves a friend of Franco'.[67]

Transport House were jubilant indeed. They stigmatised the CP
policy as a return of the Lib-Lab politics of the last century (as indeed
it was), and argued forcefully that the Popular Front would bring
nothing but disadvantages for Labour, even on the electoral level:

> 'We cannot accept the assumption that, in present circumstances,
> such a combination, even if it were practicable, would lead to the
> early defeat or break-up of the "National" Government. On the
> contrary, we believe that there is an increasing probability of a
> Labour victory in the next election, and that such a victory would
> be hindered by the building up of an artifical combination,
> ineffective and embarrassing to its parties and unlikely to impress
> the bulk of the electorate.'[68]

This was true as far as it went (and further by-election results were to confirm it), but the most fundamental objection to the whole concept came from the past history of the movement. The greatest single step in the previous history of the British working class had been the abandonment of the loose relationship of the trade unions with the Liberal Party, their acceptance of the necessity for the independence of Labour, and the embodiment of this principle in a party of their own, resting upon their own institutions. Such a lesson enters deeply into the consciousness of a class, and no matter how hard learned, cannot easily be forgotten. As the ILP pointed out, 'all those who know the record of the Liberal Party and its leaders and how they have betrayed the workers on every critical issue must raise their voices to reaffirm the need for working class and Socialist Independence'.[69] For their part, the Communists knew what they were doing. Palme Dutt put his finger right on the matter when he wrote that 'it would be a mistake to under-estimate the sincere difficulties and misgivings felt by many Labour supporters with regard to the proposal of a People's Front, which is still widely misunderstood as if it were a reversion of the old type of right wing Liberal-Labour policy'.[70]

The Communists had an elaborate rationale for this retrograde and disruptive orientation. Their reply to the NEC of the Labour Party, issued on May 21st, tried to maintain that it was 'entirely misleading to draw any analogy with the experience of the Labour Governments of 1924 and 1929, and their relations with the *Liberal Party*. Both Labour and Liberals were elected on programmes that had nothing in common. A People's Government can only be elected on the basis of a *common programme*, which all who support, are pledged loyally to carry out'.[71] Questions such as who was to frame this programme and enforce it upon its constituents were left suspended between earth and heaven, in the same way that a 'People's Government' would float between the opposing classes. All the structure of the Marxist analysis of politics, of the state apparatus, of the role of the fundamental classes, of the relationship of these with the political parties, and of the mechanics of government was jettisoned as so much unwanted ballast from this hot-air powered contraption. And balancing precariously as the whole thing did solely on the need to create a government that would ally with the Soviet Union, it is not surprising that Labour preferred to travel its old ways—and alone. All the arts of the Communists failed to get it off the ground:

'The Communist Party gives place to no one in acknowledging

the indebtedness of the whole Labour Movement to the old pioneers who at street corners, in the trades unions and workshops, fought and suffered for their advocacy of an independent Labour movement. It was a struggle that had to be fought against Liberalism in particular. That struggle was successful and an independent Labour Movement has been established with its basic principles.

But at this moment the whole future of the Labour Movement is at stake and unless the unity of all those who want to prevent Fascism and war is achieved, we are all faced with the loss of all that was gained by Labour pioneers.'[72]

The coming war was the strongest card in the CP hand, and they played it repeatedly. In the conditions of crisis that marked the last year before the world drifted to war, it was just not enough to pin the hopes of the movement on the possibility of a Labour election victory some time in the indeterminate future. The National Government rested upon too large a majority to be dislodged in by-elections alone, and a General Election need not come up until 1940. Only a split within the ruling class could bring it down. The Communists were staking everything on the withdrawal of support by patriotic Tories from the Chamberlain administration. 'But the Labour Party statement still rejects the People's Front. It still stands for the division of forces opposed to Chamberlain', they complained: 'Had the Labour Party taken the lead in mobilising the United Peace Alliance, the Chamberlain Government could have been swept from power and a People's Government put in its place.'[73]

What their calculation had missed is that patriotic Tories were more bellicose than Chamberlain's appeasers in their aims of maintaining Britain's prestige in Europe and its Empire abroad, and their accession to power in any shape or form would be more likely to lead to war than to prevent it. All a Popular Front Government would do was to paralyse the resistance of the working class, accelerating Hitler's victory as in Spain in 1936-9 and in France in 1940. The only way the Chamberlain government could have been removed was by a united offensive of the working class (which the Communists had done their best to split up), using a co-ordination of industrial and political weapons. They were right to insist upon the need for an alliance, but wrong on its class basis. As the ILP affirmed, 'We need an alliance to oppose the National Government. But it must be an alliance, not of workers and capitalists, but of workers and workers.'[74] It was quite beside the point for the CP to describe the Popular Front as 'in no way an abandonment of Socialism, but . . .'

the essential method of preserving the very possibility of an advance to Socialism',[75] for the precondition for Socialist change must be a united workers' movement, acting consciously in independence of other classes.

The importance of the Aylesbury by-election was that it proclaimed this message loud and clear, helping to turn the tide against the People's Front. A resolution in favour of the 'United Peace Alliance' was turned down at the annual Co-operative congress in June by 4,492,000 votes to 2,382,000, and the National Conferences of the Labour Women and the National Union of Railwaymen threw it out at the same time. For a while the pressure against Labour eased up, only to return with renewed force at the Munich crisis in September. The breathing space was put to good use by the NEC in pressurising local parties to withdraw their support for the Popular Front campaign, even to the extent of disaffiliating recalcitrants and those too thoroughly permeated by CP entrists.

The Munich crisis marked a fresh stage in the Communist pressure upon Labour for a People's Front. They were considerably assisted in October by a seat falling vacant in Oxford, long a stronghold of the CP through their support among student circles. (These university circles, especially in Cambridge, were to provide the Soviet Union with agents planted in British intelligence in the post-war period.) So strong was their influence in the Oxford party, that against the advice of the Labour NEC, they persuaded the candidate, Patrick Gordon Walker, to stand down, and ran instead another Labour supporter, A. D. Lindsay, the Master of Balliol, who was willing to stand as an 'Independent Progressive' on a Popular Front programme, and prevent the Liberals putting up a candidate. Although the Tory vote was cut by some three thousand, Lindsay was defeated by Quintin Hogg, and it is hard to believe that abstention by traditional Labour supporters did not contribute to the result.

A month later brought another by-election, this time at Bridgewater in Somerset. The Communists got the local divisional Labour Party not to stand and to allow a free run for the Liberal candidate, *News Chronicle* reporter Vernon Bartlett, a Popular Fronter who promised not to take a party whip. George Strauss rendered considerable support to their strategy by getting 39 Labour MPs to sign a letter of support to Bartlett, who won the seat. But this sort of thing could only lead to the revival of the dying Liberal Party in the rural districts, and to the demoralisation and liquidation of the Labour parties there. It was not part of the Communist plan actually to destroy the Labour Party, only to bind it hand and foot in a multi-class bloc, and they realised the dangers of the political tight-rope that they were treading. On November 9th, 1938, they issued a political letter explaining that:

> 'While it is highly important that all possible steps should be taken in the localities to prevent the splitting of the anti-Government vote, a widespread movement for the withdrawal of Labour candidates in favour of Independents as the only method of achieving a common front would be manifestly disastrous; and the importance of the local examples of this process is principally as evidence of the desire for unity and the dangers arising from a continued refusal of unity by headquarters.'[76]

In other words, the attack upon divisional Labour parties in the country was to blackmail Transport House into accepting the Popular Front policy at a National level, on pain of losing its future possibilities of office; but the party as a whole had to be kept in existence to ensure the subordination of the working class to a future 'People's Government'.

Other Parties came in for the same sort of treatment. In December 1938 the Duchess of Atholl, a Tory, resigned from the Conservatives over the Government's foreign policy, and resigned also her seat in Perth to fight a by-election over the issue. She was the ideal candidate to split the Tories on patriotic lines, as well as being an incorrigible fellow traveller of the CP. She had been one of the star turns at the Second National Conference of 'Peace and Friendship with the Soviet Union' in March 1937, along with such celebrities as Eleanor Rathbone and the Red Dean of Canterbury. In June 1938 she had published a book retailing the specially doctored Communist view of the Spanish Civil War, openly approving of their rôle in the 'return to order' in the counter-revolution behind the republican lines.[77] Like any other good Tory, she was willing to lay aside her own anti-Communist prejudices to be able to assist in a similar operation should the situation arise here.

She had plenty of prejudices to lose. The Communists themselves had denounced her during the bad old 'class against class' days for supporting child Labour,[78] and calling for a boycott of Soviet goods,[79] or for high tariffs to keep them out.[80] They had attacked her for supporting a joint campaign of several religious bodies against the atheism of 'Bolshevik Communist propaganda', along with 'her troupe of earls, archbishops, Rt. Revs., Revs., Vens., Rt. Hons. and what-nots'[81] the very people that the Communists were falling over themselves to recruit into their circles of 'peace and friendship' now that they had suddenly discovered that the Soviet Union was realising 'several of the most important teachings of our Master'.

That was all past history, and Communist Party support for them was enthusiastic now. In the Duchess' case they made little attempt even to gloss over her position with a 'progressive' veneer. 'We consider that all who who are against the Government's foreign policy should support her candidature', announced Kerrigan on behalf of the Scottish District Committee of the CP.[82] As Labour had no organisation in the constituency, it fell to the Liberals to turn the fight into a three-cornered one, and to earn a lecture from the editorial staff of the *Daily Worker* on their lack of patriotism for doing so.

'It is extremely unfortunate that the Liberal has decided to stand. But there can be no sacrifice too great in the struggle against those who are selling our country to German and Italian Fascism. The Duchess realises this . . . Is it too much to ask the Liberals to realise this? If they now place country above party and withdraw their candidate, the Duchess will be returned on a policy no different from that to which all true Liberals subscribe.'[83]

It was an interesting admission on the part of those who had so lately denied that the 'United Peace Alliance' was a return to Liberal Politics (in this instance the politics that took Britain into the First World War, as opposed to the older Liberalism of Gladstone and Campbell Bannerman). In effect, what it meant, was that the Communists had progressed from dictating to the Labour Party from the right, to doing the same for the Liberals.

Neither the support of Communists, nor that of a score of Labour MPs, affected the result very much, and the Duchess was beaten by her Tory opponent. Labour's prophecy that the Popular Front would prove an embarrassment to the parties involved in it proved all too true. A string of by-elections in the following year made the point clearer. In Southwark North and Kennington Labour took the seat from the Government's nominees, a Tory and a 'National'Liberal respectively, and at Aston, whilst they failed to carry the seat, they cut the Conservative majority by four thousand votes. At Brecon and Radnor Labour defeated the Tories by 2,636 votes, and in the Colne Valley the Labour vote rocketed while the Conservative vote fell. But at Westminster Abbey the Popular Front nominee, an 'Independent Progressive' called Carritt, was soundly thrashed by the Tories on the lowest poll since 1918. It was obvious that Labour's support turned out on a class basis, and it was not transferred to those who had no class allegiance, no matter how 'Progressive' they might claim to be. In any case, Carritt's brand of progress was made quite clear when he stood on a purely

Communist Party ticket in the elections of 1945,[84] and was shortly afterwards elected on to the Party's executive.[85]

It was plain that the Popular Front meant suicide for the Labour Party. As A. V. Alexander, leader of the Co-op Party remarked to his annual Conference on April 8th,

> 'Those who support the Peace Alliance have not the wisdom of election strategy. We are convinced that the United Peace Alliance, instead of being an electoral asset, is a liability.' (*Tribune*, 14th April, 1939.)

By this time war was on the way, with the Chamberlain government still refusing to sign a military pact with the Soviet Union, and the Communists and their allies becoming increasingly desperate. It was especially the case with Sir Stafford Cripps, who had told Dalton at the time of the Munich crisis that 'he would put Socialism aside for the present', and that 'the Labour Party alone could never win'. On the 13th January, 1939 he submitted a memorandum on the Popular Front to the NEC of the Labour Party, which they rejected by 17 votes to 3. He reacted wildly by circulating it along with a stamped addressed reply envelope to all Labour MPs, prospective candidates and the secretaries of affiliated organisations, flatly refusing to withdraw it when the NEC called upon him to do so. On the 25th January they expelled him from the executive by a vote of 17 to 1, and justified their decision in a statement and two pamphlets, *Socialism or Surrender?* and *Unity True or Sham*. They described Cripps' action as 'an organised and privately financed campaign in support of a programme of his own manufacture', a programme, moreover, 'from which all Socialist proposals have been eliminated', and 'a reversion to Liberalism'. A side-swipe at the Popular Front Policy analysed it as 'a pure Liberal policy' that was asking the Labour Party to 'merge its independence in an ill-defined coalition of parties and groups having little in common except their opposition to the Government's foreign policy'.

They affirmed their own loyalty to Socialism, and taunted Cripps with his previous leftism. They clinched the argument with the assertion that 'without a bold application of Socialist principles there is no escape from many of our most pressing difficulties'.[86] When the campaign went on they showed their determination on March 22nd, 1939 by expelling from the party Cripps and his closest allies, Aneurin Bevan, George Strauss, C. P. Trevelyan and Commander Edgar Young (prospective parliamentary candidate for Hull North West). While Cripps and the MPs later made their peace with the party, Young remained a Communist sympathiser without a party card, to render outside support to their political initiatives later.

Again the issue came before the Labour Party Conference that met at Southport at the end of May 1939. Cripps was allowed to speak in the debate to refer back that section of the report dealing with his expulsion (though technically no longer a member), but he was effectively countered by Dalton's speech on the necessity for minorities to behave in a disciplined manner and to accept majority decisions, and the reference back was lost on a vote of 2,100,000 to 402,000. Clearly, if every NEC member were allowed to start his private campaigns on behalf of other political parties, there was very little point in having a Labour party at all, and still less point in holding conferences to thrash out its policies. The case for the Popular Front itself was put by J. T. Murphy, arguing that 'the immediate choice before the people in this party is not that of Capitalism versus Socialism', but 'a choice between the continued existence of the pro-Fascist Chamberlain Government and the advance towards Socialism through the preservation of Democracy, of peace, and of our liberty'.[87] Once more Morrison rose to demolish him; the way forward for traditional Liberals, and sincere and enlightened people among the Conservatives, he said, was to line up behind the Labour Party—not to support a multi-party bloc of irreconcilables that threatened to create confusion by coming apart at any time. He explained how parties depending upon different classes cannot operate together in a viable alliance, as well as teaching the political lesson of modern times—that leadership of the struggle for dignity, liberty and progress was now in the hands of the working class. The message was so clear that the motion fell by an even wider margin—2,360,000 votes to 248,000.[88] The trade unions remained, as always, adamant on the question. When the Railwaymen debated it a month later, their General Secretary described it as 'putting Socialism into cold storage and leading to political disaster', and it was rejected by 53 delegates' votes to 26.[89]

The arguments used by the mainstream of the Labour movement to defend its position at this period provide an object lesson for those who see politics in facile and self-applied labels of 'Left', 'Right' or 'Moderate'. The Labour and trade union leadership were put in the position of having to draw upon class struggle arguments to preserve their political basis against an inter-class onslaught articulated by Communists. When they described the Popular Front as 'merely the old policy of class collaboration under a new name' the Communists replied that this was a 'stock argument used by the Right Wing pseudo-Left Trotskyist combination',[90] 'empty and meaningless talk of a future fight for Socialism on the part of those who refuse to lead the fight on the burning issues of today'.[91] But behind this attempt to tar the Labour leaders with the brush of 'Trotskyism' lay the haunting realisation that the logic of events had reversed their relative positions, leaving Labour free to wield the old class war weapons against the Communists.

The Communists on their part were only too glad to surrender them. A Central Committee resolution of 1937, justified the dropping of the idea of the dictatorship of the proletariat by the 'need to make it clear that this issue is not now on the order of the day in the present situation in Britain', and anyway, in the first place, it had only meant 'a very broad form of democracy for the working people'. January 1938 saw the slogan 'Workers of All Lands Unite' dropped from the masthead of the *Daily Worker*. The Communists led no more mass demonstrations of the unemployed movement after 1936, even though unemployment persisted at over a million a year until 1940. The Movement's leader, Wal Hannington, was even removed from the Central Committee after an obscure quarrel over finance.

It is odd for us to remember that this was the Communist Party's heroic period, and it has dined out on the reputation of it ever since. Now, after nearly fifty years, it is becoming plain that the party's stand on some of these issues was by no means as clear as it has claimed. Joe Jacobs, an activist in the East End anti-fascist movement, has shown that to begin with the Communists had no intention of stopping Mosely in the great mobilisation in Cable Street. His book, *Out of the Ghetto* (London, 1978, pp 235 ff) describes how to begin with they had organised a YCL meeting in Trafalgar Square to support the Spanish Republican Government at the time that Mosely had planned his march and two local meetings arranged in the area for the same time had been given instructions to let Mosely's march go through, and avoid clashes and disorder. Only after repeated protest from the activists in the East End did the London District Committee of the CP change its arrangements, under threat of losing its local members. It was not that the Party's leaders were lacking in either courage or anti-fascist feeling, but the Popular Front line predisposed them to respectable protest rather than direct militant action, which could only antagonise those they were so anxious to influence among the Tories, Liberals and 'Progressives'.

Its corollary was the increased attention paid to the party's middle and upper class periphery. During the 1920s, for example the Communist Party had been so anti-'intellectual' that it had used it as a term of abuse to secure a condemnation of Trotskyism from its largely working class rank and file.[92] As late as 1934 Gallacher could think of no worse insult to level at Trotsky than that he was 'a petty bourgeois Liberal', infected with 'rotten Liberalism'.[93] But Gallacher was now appealing to 'shopkeepers and the whole wide range of professional people who are identified with Liberalism or associated with peace organisations'.[94] Those who had been seen as such mortal enemies during the 'Third Period' were suddenly transformed by legerdemain into staunch allies of the workers in their struggle for Peace and Democracy:

> 'Teachers, doctors, and other professional workers, small shop-keepers and traders, small farmers and market gardeners, civil servants and local government officials, scientific workers and intellectuals generally can be brought to realise that their own interests are harmed by the interests of the millionaires and the millionaires' National Government.'[95]

No attempt was made to follow this logic through to its conclusion, that if capitalist democracy benefitted so narrow a section of the community, then the time had come to overthrow it in the interests of everybody else. For the Communists were interested in the middle classes maintaining their illusions, not shedding them. The middle class element accordingly shot up within the party in proportion to its moves towards the right.[96]

Yet substantial advances were made into the trades unions at the same time. Many class conscious workers believed that the Communists' campaign for affiliation to the Labour Party was a turn in the direction of the labour movement, and not an attempt to undermine it on behalf of other classes. They saw the rank and file CP supporter for what he was, a brave and dedicated fighter for trade union rights and organisation. If CP party headquarters saw this only as another weapon in the fight to undermine the National Government, that was no concern of theirs. By a determined drive to unionise engineering factories, for example, the Communist Party earned their strong position inside the union, in particular in the London area.

Many joined the party under the mistaken impression that its label of 'Communist' actually did mean something, and that they were entering the party that stood for the class struggle. Support came also from other quarters, for less creditable motives. Communists combined with partizans of the notorious 'Black Circular', against militants who opposed the 'Popular Front' alliance with the Liberals and Tories, sometimes with ludicrous results.[97] On other occasions the multitude of fellow travellers, crypto Communists and 'Progressives' made it almost impossible to sort out who stood for what.[98] Whatever the result, on the shop floor it often seemed that the Labour leaders opposed the National Government in words, whilst the Communists did so in deeds.

The forces to which the Communists were specially anxious to appeal were much further to the right, and no effort was spared to cater to their prejudices. Those who had believed religion to be the opiate of the people, and had filled their newspapers in the twenties with trenchant criticism of it, now asked the working class to 'welcome the progressive tendencies that are showing themselves in certain religious organisations'.[99] Despite the well-known role of Lutheranism and Catholicism under Hitler (and Dollfüss and Mussolini) the Communists were trying to prove that 'among protestants and catholics there is uneasiness at the brutal and repressive methods that fascism adopts to prevent religious teaching and expression, and resentment that Chamberlain's policy helps the fascists to carry through their attack upon religion by force'.[100] They were especially anxious to include clerics and ministers on pro-Soviet platforms and their congregations in front organisations for 'peace'.[101] 'More especially do I appeal to the Catholic Church', pleaded Willie Gallacher for 'too long have some of its influential leaders assisted the Fascist aggressors by their wicked support of the invasion of Spain . . .'[102]

His appeal fell on deaf ears, with good reason. Religion supplied much support for Nazi and Fascist governments. In Spain (in particular) the enthusiasm of the church for Franco's 'Crusade' was not unconnected with its vast capital holdings, at one time reckoned at a third of the national total for one religious order alone.[103]

Evidently the followers of the Prince of Peace were less firm in their commitment to it than the Communist leaders. Alliance with them was all the more remarkable, as for years the CP had supported the view that the support of the workers for peace had a different character from that of the middle and upper class pacifists whom they were now wooing. As Lenin pointed out,

'The sentiments of the masses in favour of peace often express incipient protest, anger and consciousness of the reactionary character of the war. It is the duty of all socialists to utilise these sentiments. They will take a most ardent part in every movement and in every demonstration on this ground; *but they will not deceive the people by conceding the idea that peace without annexations, without the oppression of nations, without plunder, without the germs of new wars among the present governments and ruling classes is possible in the absence of a revolutionary movement.*'[104]

The illusions Lenin scorned so fiercely were exactly those of the CPGB in its Popular Front days. It involved them in an immense reversal of their attitudes towards pacifists within and outside the labour movement. The traditional spokesman for Labour's pacifism inside the movement, the Christian Socialist George Lansbury, was transformed from being a promoter of the 'line of fascism'[105] to 'a respected veteran of the movement'.[106] The party's press moved from denouncing him for supporting the League of Nations 'to give the impression that it is working for peace, instead of being a sort of Executive of the joint imperialist powers',[107] to condemning equally vehemently those who made 'attacks upon and efforts to disrupt the local Peace Councils as they support "bourgeois" collective security'.[108]

But then, as the party press never ceased to explain, the League of Nations and 'Collective Security' had undergone a change since the Soviet Union came into them. From being 'a powerful instrument of war against which the workers must unceasingly struggle',[109] the League became necessary because 'only a common stand of the democratic powers can save peace'.[110] The idea that the League was 'a body genuinely anxious to work for peace' went from being 'the most dangerous of all illusions'[111] to something perfectly acceptable, even to the point of backing its 'economic and military sanctions if necessary'.[112]

It is a shorter step (than most people think) in class terms, from bourgeois pacifism to full support for imperialist war. Most of the worst wars of recent times have been fought against this or that state that was 'breaking the peace', the prime example being 'the war to end all wars'. The world of 1938-9 was full of talk about peace and the necessity for it, while frantic rearmament went on all over the place. As the old saying goes, when the ruling class talk about peace, it means they are preparing for another war. Once the British Communist Party had taken the step towards pacifism, and then the League of Nations and Collective Security, the next logical progression was in the direction of support for war preparations, and outright chauvinism. The approaching crisis admitted of no middle position, and events were urging the British Communists forwards, however reluctantly. During the old 'Third Period' days Andrew Rothstein had been repeating the Leninist position that the best contribution the workers could make to peace would be the overthrow of their own government, even if Germany were attacking Russia and Britain had come into the war against Germany.[113] Revolutionary defeatism on both sides was to be the policy equally in the event of a war between Fascist Germany and Fascist Poland.[114] Now the CP's only objection to compulsory national service in the coming war was that the military alliance between Britain and France did not include the Soviet Union on equal terms. *'It is morally indefensible'*, they went on, *'that the agreements don't include the Soviet Union.* We say again—let Britain make such an agreement, decide what forces are necessary and youth will voluntarily fulfil its obligations.'[115]

It was a short hop from there to alliance with the war-mongering wing of the Tory party. Whereas before they had limited themselves to the position that 'neither the vested interests of Labour nor Liberal leaders should be allowed to stand in the way of organising them in the People's Front',[116] now they went the whole way in the direction of the Churchill ramp of the Conservatives, the bitterest enemies of the labour movement. As Pollitt was to express it,

> 'Surely it is a matter of political interest that inside the ranks of the great powerful Tory party cracks are appearing; powerful leaders of conservatism in this country openly declare that Chamberlain is sacrificing the interests of Britain. This is not something to cry about. It is something to encourage, to stimulate, whatever the motives may be.'[117]

The method used to 'stimulate' these elements was to throw all caution to the winds and indulge in the purest chauvinism. When a picture of Chamberlain appeared in a local Conservative HQ shop window at the time of Munich, the party noted with approval that 'what angered most people was that Chamberlain should be smugly draped round the flag he had done so much to dishonour'.[118] Outbidding the National Government in patriotism, they accused it of 'threatening communications vital to British interests';[119] and the culmination of the People's Front was encapsulated in the remark that 'The struggle of the British people against the Chamberlain government is a struggle for its very existence as a democratic and unconquered people'.[120] Even when they drew back from the worst consequences of their policies, such as conscription, the Communist Party could not avoid injecting into it a dose of nationalism, describing it as 'the destruction of English liberties'.[121]

There was nothing left now to prevent the British Communist Party becoming an expression of extreme chauvinism. A leaflet given out at a rally in Hyde Park captured the essence of it:

> 'England! A word of power. A name deeply engraved on the minds of men, whether murmured with love, whispered in fear . . .
> A people with a great history, great achievements, great

traditions, etc . . .'

This was not an expression of the spirits of a raw rank and file, of newcomers who had joined the communist movement in ignorance of its basic principles. Their most self-conscious theoretician, R. Page Arnot, quoted it to the effect that 'liberty is the noble tradition of England, and liberty won by the struggle of class against class.' Running through an eulogy of British poets, philosophers and scientists, he boosted the leaflet with enthusiastic approval. As he put it,

'The Communists have claimed their rightful place in the great tradition, the heritage which is theirs.'[122]

Indeed. And there we must leave them for the present chapter; after having been more Labour than Labour, and then more Liberal than the Liberals, they had finally ended up being more Tory than the Tories.

Footnotes

1 *Controversy*, June 1937, p. 42.
2 Gollancz in the *New Leader*, vol. xxi, new series no. 178, 11th June, 1937.
3 *New Statesman and Nation*, 4th September, 1937.
4 *Daily Worker*, 25th July, 1931.
5 *Daily Worker*, 22nd January, 1937.
6 *Daily Worker*, 19th February, 1937: 'When I wrote the book, the trial had just begun . . . I prejudged . . . I read the rest of the evidence and became convinced there was a gigantic plot against the Soviet government . . . it was too late to alter the book . . .'
7 'Mrs. Sidney Webb Supports the Means Test', in the *Daily Worker*, 14th November, 1931.
8 'Workers' Notebook: Beatrice Webb', in the *Daily Worker*, 24th January, 1938: 'If I were to set out to make a list of all she has done for the Labour movement in this country, it would fill many notebooks. But this is not necessary. The finest thing that one can say of her is that she has never grown old or rested on her laurels.'
9 *News Chronicle*, editorial columns of 20th May, 1937 and 15th March, 1938.
10 H. Pollitt, Report on 'Economic Security, Peace, and Democracy', in *For Peace and Plenty*, the Report of the 15th Congress of the CPGB, p. 83.
11 *Labour Party Conference Report*, 1936, p. 50.
12 'British Labour and Communism', in the *Labour Party Conference Report*, 1936, pp. 296-300.
13 *Labour Party Conference Report*, p. 257.

14 *Op. cit.*, p. 208.
15 E. Bevin, 'Labour Stands Firm', in the T&GWU 'Record', December, 1938.
16 C. Attlee, *The Labour Party in Perspective*, London, 1937, p. 123 and 124.
17 Presidential address by W. Gallacher M.P. in *For Peace and Plenty*, Report of the 15th Congress of the CPGB, p. 12.
18 'Discussion: Towards the 15th Party Congress of the CP', in the *Daily Worker*, 11th July, 1938.
19 'The Soviet Trial', in *Labour Monthly*, vol. xviii, no. 10, October 1936, p. 618.
20 *Daily Worker*, 24th August, 1936.
21 *Daily Worker*, 3rd February, 1937.
22 'D. N. Pritt K.C. Advises Daily Herald—Do Not Play the Game of Reaction', in the *Daily Worker*, 19th July, 1937.
23 *Daily Worker*, 25th January, 1937.
24 *Daily Worker*, 12 August, 1937.
25 *Ibid.*
26 Frank Pitcairn, (Claude Cockburn), 'These Enemies of the People', in the *Labour Monthly*, vol. xx, no. 1, January, 1938, p. 25.
27 'Moscow Trial. "No Time for Sentiment" ', in the *Daily Worker*, 28th August, 1936, p. 3. *Cf.* 'Report of the Central Committee to the 15th Party Congress of the CPGB', 16th-19th September, 1938, p. 54.
28 F. Brockway, *Workers' Front*, London, 1938, p. 234; H. J. Laski, in the New York 'Nation', 20th November, 1937, *cf.* the New Leader *14th January, 1938*.
29 *The Labour Party and the Popular Front*, May, 1938, *cf.* below, p. 39
30 *Cf.* the *Daily Worker*, 27th September and 3rd October, 1932.
31 R. Palme Dutt in *Labour Monthly*, June 1934.
32 *Daily Worker*, 15th June, 1935.
33 *Daily Worker*, 5th February, 1936.
34 'What the S.L. is doing', in *The Socialist Leaguer*, no. 12, June 1935, p. 196.
35 *The Socialist*, New Series, no. 2, November 1935, p. 8.
36 *Cf.* Jack Winnocour, 'Spain has Lighted a Torch', in *The Socialist*, New Series, 11, October, 1936, p. 5; Reg Groves, 'After the French Socialist Congress', in *The Socialist Leaguer*, no. 13, July/August, 1935, p. 214. Articles by Groves appear in practically every issue of *The Socialist*. Pamphlets written by him for the League include *Arms and the Unions* and *Trades Councils in the Fight for Socialism*.
37 Stafford Cripps, *National Fascism in Britain*. Socialist League, 1935.
38 Sir Stafford Cripps, *Can Socialism Come By Constitutional Means?*
39 Reg Groves, 'A Disclaimer', in *The Socialist Broadsheet*, no. 1, Feb-April 1937, p. 1.
40 'Attack on Unity by Trotskyist Through Columns of Daily Herald', in the *Daily Worker*, 18th January, 1937.
41 *Reynolds News*, 4th April, 1937.
42 'The Labour Party and the so-called "Unity Campaign" ', *Conference Report*, 1937, p. 27.
43 N.E.C. *Report to Conference*, 1937.
44 Op. cit., p. 163. Cf. the report by Jenny Lee in *The New Leader*, 8th October, 1937.
45 'S.L. Decision: Crushing Defeat of Trotskyists', in the *Daily Worker*, 18th May, 1937.
46 Fenner Brockway, *Inside the Left*, London, 1942, p. 268.
47 Groves, Interview with Al Richardson, 2nd April, 1978: 'But I learned afterwards, in fact fairly recently from Michael Foot, that at Pollitt's suggestion they had planned that the Socialist League be wound up; then, again at the CP's suggestion, they wound up the Unity Campaign to save the individuals from

expulsion from the Labour Party so that they could support Communist affiliation to the Labour Party'. *Cf.* Dewar, pp. 111-2, and Brockway, above, n. 46, and below, p. 35.
48 'Peace Fronts', in *Tribune*, 14th April, 1938.
49 *New Leader*, 4th June, 1937.
50 Brockway, *op. cit.*, p. 269.
51 F. Brockway, 'The Communists and Unity', in the *New Leader*, new series, no. 200, 12th November, 1937.
52 F. Brockway, *Inside the Left*, London, 1942, pp. 269-70.
53 Hugo Dewar, *Communist Politics in Britain*, London, 1976, p. 111.
54 *Labour Organiser*, November, 1936.
55 Charlotte Haldane, *Truth Will Out*, 1949, pp. 182-266.
56 Douglas Hyde, *I Believed*, London, 1950, pp. 64-66.
57 'Labour Youth Meets', in the *Militant*, vol. ii. no. 6, January, 1939, p. 4.
58 'Who Publishes Youth Militant and Why?', in the *Youth Militant*, new series no. 1, December, 1939, p. 3; *Daily Worker*, 14th July, 1939.
59 *Daily Worker*, 7th, 13th, 19th, and 20th July, and 11th and 31st August, 1939.
60 *A.R.P. The Practical Air Raid Protection Britain Needs*, CPGB pamphlet, 18th July, 1938 (emphasis as in original).
61 *No Conscription; But Free Volunteers for a Collective Peace Policy*, CPGB pamphlet (undated).
62 Reg Groves, interview with Al Richardson, 2nd April, 1978.
63 R. Palme Dutt, 'The People's Front is the Door to Socialism', in the *Daily Worker*, 14th May, 1938.
64 'Now for a Workers' Front', in the *New Leader*, vol. xxxii, new series, no. 228, 27th May, 1938.
65 John Strachey, 'The Peace Alliance Holds the Field', in *Labour Monthly*, vol. xx, no. 7, July, 1938, p. 417.
66 *Daily Herald*, 21st May, 1938.
67 'Aylesbury Result a Free Gift to Government', in the *Daily Worker*, 21st May, 1938.
68 *The Labour Party and the Popular Front*, Statement of the N.E.C. on the 'United Peace Alliance'.
69 'Support Labour at Aylesbury', in the *New Leader*, vol. xxxi, new series, no. 226, 13th May, 1938, p. 2.
70 R. Palme Dutt, 'Notes of the Month', in *Labour Monthly*, vol. xx, no. 6, June, 1938, p. 336.
71 *The People's Front*, Statement of the CC of the CPGB, 21st May, 1938, pp. 124-5 (emphasis in original).
72 *Op. cit.*, p. 126.
73 *Op. cit.*, p. 123.
74 'Support Labour at Aylesbury', in the *New Leader*, new series, vol. xxxi, no. 226, 13th May, 1938, p. 2.
75 *Letter to All Organisations affiliated to the Labour Party*, CPGB, 8th June, 1938, p. 135.
76 *Political Letter to the CP Membership*, CPGB, 9th November 1938, p. 4.
77 Duchess of Atholl, *Searchlight on Spain*, June 1938, especially ch. xxi, pp. 165-173, 'The Return to Order'.
78 'The Independent Duchess', in the *Daily Worker*, 18th September, 1930.
79 *Daily Worker*, 12th November, 1931.
80 'Commons Attack on Soviet Union', in the *Daily Worker*, 18th February, 1932.
81 'The Duchess Again', in the *Daily Worker*, 3rd January, 1935 (described prophetically and sarcastically as 'our old friend'!)

82 'Rebel Duchess May shake the Government', in the *Daily Worker*, 5th December, 1938.
83 'No Sacrifice Too Great', in the *Daily Worker*, 26th November, 1938.
84 *World News and Views*, vol. xxv, no. 21, 2nd June, 1945.
85 *Communist Policy for Britain*, Report of the 18th Congress of the Communist Party, 24th November, 1945.
86 *Labour and the Popular Front*, in the *Daily Worker*, 3rd February, 1939, p. 4.
87 *Labour Party Annual Conference Report*, 1939, p. 293.
88 *Ibid*.
89 'Railmen and the Popular Front', in the *Daily Worker*, 8th July, 1939.
90 J. R. Campbell, 'The Trotskyist Danger', in *For Peace and Plenty*, Report of the 15th Congress of the CPGB, September, 1938, p. 99.
91 *The People's Front*, Statement of the CC of the CPGB, 21st May, 1938, pp. 127-8.
92 C. M. Roebuck (Rothstein), 'Trotskyism—A Peril to the Party','in *Workers Weekly*, 23rd January, 1926, p. 5; cf. R. Page Arnot's speech in 'A Splendid rally of London Members. Keen Discussion on Trotsky', in the same issue, p. 6.
93 W. Gallacher, *Pensioners of Capitalism*, CPGB pamphlet, 1934, p. 7.
94 W. Gallacher's Presidential Address in *For Peace and Plenty*, Report of the 15th Congress of the CPGB, September 1938, p. 15.
95 14th Congress of the CPGB, 29-31 May, 1937.
96 K. Newton, *The Sociology of British Communism*, 1969, pp. 21, 42-53. The highest membership figure recorded for the thirties was 17,756, attained in July, 1939.
97 'Vigilant', 'Communists and the Black Circular', in the *New Leader*, 11th March, 1938.
98 'Railmen and the Popular Front', in the *Daily Worker*, 8th July, 1939 (Speech by Marchbank, General Secretary of the NUR).
99 'The Religious Organisations and Peace', in *For Peace and Plenty*, p. 150.
100 Harry Pollitt in *Labour Monthly*, October, 1938.
101 'Worker's Notebook', 'Big British Support for World Peace Congress. 100 Organisations Now Affiliated to National Committee', in the *Daily Worker*, 17th October, 1938.
102 W. Gallacher, Presidential Address in *For Peace and Plenty*, September 1938, p. 16.
103 *Cf*., the references given in G. Brennan, *The Spanish Labyrinth*, Cambridge 1943, pp 46-7.
104 Lenin (and Zinoviev), *Socialism and War*, Peking Edition, pp. 26-7 (our emphasis).
105 R. Palme Dutt in *Labour Monthly*, June, 1934.
106 A. Hutt, *The Post-War History of the British Working Class*, London, 1937, p. 234.
107 *Daily Worker*, 17th February, 1932.
108 H. Pollitt, Report on 'Economic Security, Peace and Democracy', in *For Peace and Plenty*, September, 1938, p. 70.
109 W. Rust, 'The League is Not Impotent', in the *Daily Worker*, 19th February, 1932.
110 Reply of the Editorial Board to Brailsford, in the *Daily Worker*, 15th January, 1938, cf. J. R. Campbell, *Questions and Answers on Communism*, CPGB pamphlet, March 1938, p. 41.
111 'Maxton and the League', in the *Daily Worker*, 19th February, 1932. The *Daily Worker*, of June 24th described the League as 'an organisation of the leading imperialist powers of the world'. For other examples of the Communist Party's attitude to the League at this time, cf. the issues of 17th, 20th and 26th February, 1932, and of *Labour Monthly* for November 1934 (R. F. Andrews—Andrew Rothstein) and January 1935 (R. Palme Dutt).

112 H. Pollitt, in *Labour Monthly*, October 1935.
113 A. Rothstein, *The Labour Party and the Menace of War*, CPGB pamphlet (n.d.)
114 J. R. Campbell, in *Labour Monthly*, September, 1933.
115 *No Conscription: But Free Volunteers for a Collective Peace Policy*, CPGB pamphlet, n.d. (emphasis as in original).
116 *The People's Front*, Statement of the CC of the CPGB, 21st May, 1938, p. 127.
117 H. Pollitt, *Defence of the People*, CPGB pamphlet, 1939, pp. 11-12.
118 'Worker's Notebook', 'Chamberlain and the Union Jack', in the *Daily Worker*, 17th October, 1938.
119 *Statement of the CC of the CPGB*, 19th March, 1938.
120 'Unity for Peace and Economic Security', the main resolution of the 15th Congress of the CPGB, in *For Peace and Plenty*, p. 139.
121 *No Conscription: but Free Volunteers for a Collective Peace Policy*, CPGB pamphlet, n.d.
122 R. Page Arnot, 'The English Tradition', in *Labour Monthly*, vol xviii, no. 11, November 1936, pp. 693-700.

Chapter Four

Beating
the Retreat,
1939-41

At last conditions had ripened for a European war. Franco entered
Barcelona on the 25th January, 1939, and a month later the British
government had accepted the legality of his regime. By the end of
March the Spanish Civil War was all over. So were the hopes of the
working class that they could halt the coming conflict by the defeat
of at least one of the dictators.

As spring turned to summer the temperature of conflict also
warmed up. By proclaiming the 'Protectorate of Bohemia and
Moravia' on the 15th March Hitler brought to an end the rump state
of Czecho-Slovakia guaranteed by the Munich signatories. As the
major powers accelerated their rearmament the smaller European
states sniffed the air for burning and showed their awareness by
making appropriate adjustments. Only eight days afterwards
Lithuania handed back to Germany Memel-land, the territory
awarded to her by the Versailles pacemakers. The great powers drew
closer their alliance systems to brace themselves for war. Germany
and Italy signed the 'Pact of Steel' on the 22nd May: France and
Britain, acting in concert now for some time, extended their alliance
by offering guarantees to Romania and Poland as the year progressed. Then, with a profound shock to the whole International
labour movement, came the announcement on the 23rd August of
the Molotov/Ribbentrop pact.

Nothing could now avoid the general conflagration, since the
secret clauses of the agreement provided for the partition of Poland
between the two states. At a quarter to five on the morning of
September 1st Hitler's tanks rolled across the Polish border. Two
days later Britain and France were at war with Germany.

As the main contenders in Western Europe, the 'democratic'
imperialists of Great Britain had marshalled their society for war in

the same way as the others. The rate of rearmament, proceeding at a more or less even tempo since 1935, suddenly quickened, and defence expenditure began to mount to dizzy heights.[1] The stock-piling of all weapons, but in particular aircraft, showed that a more central role was to be played by the civilian population than had been the case during the last war.[2] It was the message brought home by the trying on of gasmasks and air raid precaution exercises.[3] On the 27th April 1938 the government had approved aircraft production scheme L. providing for the completion of 12,000 planes inside two years, and on the 2nd February, 1939, they followed this with an authori-sation to produce 'to the limit' of capacity.

A series of shocks introduced the public to the awful realisation that another war was on the way. 38 million gasmasks had been distributed at the time of the Munich crisis; then things died down a little until March 17th, 1939, when Chamberlain announced to a cheering audience in the Birmingham Conservative Club that 'any attempt to dominate the world by force was one which the democracies must resist'.

His speech disregarded the fact that democratic Britain already dominated much of the world by force (India in particular) and when he reinforced it a month later by introducing compulsory national service he was equally oblivious of Clement Attlee's remark that 'it is very dangerous to give the generals all they want'.

Reservations about conscription were the last gestures of the leaders of the labour movement before they, too, began to take their place in the lines. Slowly, for that is the way with the bureaucracy of the labour movement, they lumbered into position behind the 'leaders of the nation'. First came a statement on 'International Policy and Defence' put out in July 1937 by the National Council of Labour that until an improvement in world circumstances, a future Labour government would not reverse rearmament until the country was strong enough to defend itself. In September the TUC gave the policy its seal of approval, to be followed a month afterwards by the Bournemouth Conference of the Labour Party. What this fanfare was meant to announce became abundantly clear when the leaders of the TUC arrived at no. 10 Downing Street, on the 23rd March, 1939 to conclude an agreement to assist rearmament by relaxing 'craft restriction' in the engineering industry. Defences fought for and elaborated by generations of engineering workers were signed away in an afternoon. The National Council of Labour chimed in with another circular at the same time to assure everyone that 'rearma-ment is necessary, and indeed unavoidable in the interests of self-defence alone'.

'National Unity' is the key to sing in when great empires go to war. The TUC remembered the tune well enough, having sung it before, when they met at the outbreak of war (1st-3rd September) and turned aside from deliberations on other matters to resolve that 'congress, with a united resolute nation, enters the struggle with a clear conscience and a steadfast purpose'.

No-one understood more than they that this meant the end of anything that stood for the independence of the Labour movement. Although Chamberlain was still in office, an electoral truce was called from the beginning of the war, though the cabinet was smaller and less representative than ever before, and Labour had as yet no place in it.

Hardships multiplied for those at the other end of the social scale. In September 1939 conscription had been extended to the whole of the male population between the ages of eighteen and forty-one. Street lighting was extinguished from the first of the month, and 1½ million schoolchildren were evacuated to the provinces from the danger areas. The beginning of the following year saw the introduction of food rationing. The imposition was spread worldwide; a staggering total of £1,138 million was extorted from the starving masses of India in a forced loan to finance the war effort, when adding insult to injury the viceroy declared war without so much as bothering to consult the façade of sham representative institutions that existed there.

The Labour Party still held back from the next step: government office. If they were to retain any credibility at all there was one concession that they had to gain: Chamberlain must go. However much official historiography may make of the speeches of Amery, Churchill, etc., the unvarnished truth is that Chamberlain's government fell because Labour made it clear that they would only take on government responsibility under a new Prime Minister. It was only when Churchill received his summons to the palace on the 10th May, 1940, that Attlee and Greenwood could agree to serve in the cabinet. Three days later Attlee gained the consent of the Labour Party Conference for this new stage in blending together the Labour Party and the state.

From that time on the official structures of the movement hardly functioned at all as bulwarks for the working class. Attlee was himself Deputy Prime Minister, in the cabinet along with Dalton, Herbert Morrison and Alexander. Most dangerous of all was the appointment of Ernest Bevin as Minister of Labour and National Services. 'Labour regulations were ignored. Men in the aircraft factories worked ten hours a day, seven days a week. Bevin counted for much in securing this new spirit of co-operation. He was determined to be dictator of Labour and enforced his position throughout the war.'[4]

His most extreme measure amounted to the militarisation of labour. Essential Work Order Regulation 58A permitted the transfer of a worker to another job, which could be in an entirely different industry at a much lower rate of pay. If he wanted to move from his current employment, he could be compelled to remain there. He could be moved, if necessary, the length of the country. To round it off, men and women unemployed before could be compelled to work, for payment or not![5] The effect of regulation 58A was to hand over full control of labour to the Minister. He, in turn, set up a National Arbitration Tribunal to make agreements on unions and employers that were compulsorily binding. Order in Council no. 1305 declared strikes and lock-outs illegal. And whilst by 1941 49% of the country's population were employed in government work of one kind or another, 'Essential Work (General Provisions) Order' of March 1941 required skilled workers to register themselves for direction into employment in the 'essential' category. As with the First World War, dilution went on unchecked, whilst industrial production rose to staggering figures: in 1941 British munitions production actually outstripped that of Nazi Germany.

In the meantime war had spread to take in most of Europe, North and East Africa, the Far East, and the oceans and skies of the world. When France signed its armistice with Germany on the 22nd June 1940, it was only a matter of time before the war came nearer home. German bombers began their attacks on South East England on August 13th, starting the bombing of London itself on the 7th September. It was an onslaught that was to continue on and off until German plans matured for the invasion of Soviet Russia in the following June.

Although the flag of national unity was draped over everything, threadbare parts still showed there was a class society beneath. When the government laid plans to send children from London's vulnerable East End overseas, shipping space was found to accommodate a mere 2,664, for no less than 21,000 women and children of the respectable classes were going at their own expense. 'Members of the government', notes A. J. P. Taylor, 'and university professors sent their families on this unseemly scramble'.[6]

Marxists repeat endlessly that war is the continuation of politics by other—more violent—means, and they see it as the supreme test for parties and their programmes. Trends that are hardly noticeable in times of peace and stability then reveal themselves in all their starkness. That had been the case with the past, and so it proved now. 'The War came, the crisis came', wrote Lenin and Zinoviev about 1914, 'Instead of revolutionary tactics, the majority of the

Social Democratic parties conducted reactionary tactics, went over to the side of their respective governments and bourgeoisie. This betrayal of Socialism signified the collapse of the Second (1889-1914) International.'[7] His words could be the epitaph of the Communist International as well.

For it is in wartime that the Marxist programme stands out in clearest contrast with all shades of reformism, which take on the colours of chauvinism, and centrism, which reveals itself as pacifist vacillation. 'Marxism is not pacifism', Lenin had explained, 'it is necessary, of course, to fight for the speediest termination of the war. But only if *revolutionary* struggle is called for does the demand for "peace" acquire proletarian meaning. Without a series of revolutions, so-called democratic peace is a philistine utopia. The purpose of a real programme of action would be served only by a *Marxian* programme, which gave the masses a full and clear explanation of what imperialism is and how to combat it, which openly stated that it was opportunism that led to the collapse of the Second International.'[8] And the Third, (we might add), including its British Section.

Alas for the British Communist Party! As soon as they managed to catch up completely with Russian policy, the 'line' began to change again. By the spring of 1939 it had already begun to alter. Stalin realised that if the Western democracies were refusing to defend Czechoslovakia (and hoping to direct the Germans against Russia into the bargain) they would certainly not go to war to defend him. For some time he had been clearing the decks for an accommodation with Hitler by damping down his aid to Spain to a trickle and slaughtering a high proportion of the agents who had done his dirty work there when they got back to the Soviet Union. Extra room for manoeuvre had been provided by his elimination of a high percentage of the Moscow-exiled leaders of the German Communist Party and his destruction of the Polish Communist Party, practically down to the last man.

As the British Communists had not been consulted about this switch it is not surprising that they failed to understand immediately what was going on. Indeed, they had got into the habit of believing it was not possible. As J. R. Campbell put it,

'The reactionary press of Britain and France has insinuated from time to time that the Soviet Union is seeking an understanding with Nazi Germany. The objective of this lying insinuation is to convince the people of the Western countries that they cannot rely on the Soviet Union for the defence of peace. It is particularly designed to convince the French people that they cannot rely on the Soviet Union to honour its obligations under the Franco-Soviet pact.

There is not an iota of fact that could be adduced in support of these insinuations, while a great mass of incontrovertible facts tell against them."[9]

If the picture was blurred at the outset, the British Communists should have been able to read the signs when the Molotov/Ribbentrop Pact was concluded. If they missed this, commonsense should have told them that Hitler's attack on Poland nine days later could only have taken place with the consent, if not the compliance, of the Soviet Union. Yet even *after* the 17th, when Stalin's own army crossed the Polish frontiers, the lessons were not entirely clear to them.

They were caught 'on the hop'. Perhaps it was due to the secrecy that shrouded the clauses in the pact concerning Poland. But a more likely explanation is that the huge influx of middle class elements into the party during the Popular Front period with their chauvinist assumptions made a quick 'about turn' extremely difficult. What is more, the party stalwarts themselves had obviously enjoyed the brief popularity of their patriotic stance.

Whatever the explanation, they hailed the pact as 'a dramatic peace move to halt aggressors':[10] then briskly chose sides affirming that 'in this war the aggressor powers are the fascist powers, Germany, Italy and Japan'.[11] At the end of August one of their entrists resigning from the Labour Party was still giving as his reason that 'the Labour leaders' attacks on the signing of the German-Soviet Pact and the surrender of Labour Party leadership to Mr. Chamberlain and his appeasement policy made it impossible to continue his work'.[12] 'Nazis plunge world into War' was the theme of the *Daily Worker* on September 2nd, accompanied by a declaration of the Central Committee 'in support of all necessary measures to secure the victory of democracy over fascism'.[13] In shorter steps, but not far behind, marched the Young Communist League, promising that 'if Fascism looses war upon the world, the YCL fully supports the policy of the CP which declares it will do all in its power to ensure a speedy victory over Fascism'.[14] To make sure the message was not missed, Willie Gallacher used the platform of the House of Commons to recommend 'the speedy defeat of Nazism as a sure way to bring about a possible hope for lasting peace'. At the same time, with more than a glance over his shoulder, he wanted to declare with the utmost confidence that he would not come into conflict with the policy of his working-class comrades of the Soviet Union.[15]

Harry Pollitt was chosen to lay down the 'Line' in a pamphlet issued on September 14th, entitled *How to Win the War*. Its message was summed up in the words that 'the Communist Party supports the war, believing it to be a just war which will be supported by the whole working class and all friends of democracy'.[16] What 'democracy' was supposed to mean here was explained by John Gollan on September the 23rd, when he wrote that 'Nazi aggression must be defeated by all the resources of the British people and the peoples of the Empire'.[17] Then suddenly, it dawned on them that their policy no longer bore the slightest resemblance to the one favoured now in Moscow. How this happened precisely is unclear, and it is difficult to say how far we are meant to take seriously the only account of it—given by a later deserter, Douglas Hyde. Nonetheless, it makes amusing reading:

> 'The Party's Central Committee had met one day at the King Street headquarters to draw up a stirring manifesto to the British people calling upon them to sacrifice all in the great anti-fascist struggle. After hours of struggle the text was finalised. Then unexpectedly, in walked the British representative to the Communist International whom everyone had thought was still in Moscow.
>
> He took one look at the manifesto, and told the leadership they would have to scrap it. It was, he said, an imperialist war. The Comintern had said so, and that meant opposing it in the classic Marxist way.
>
> Out of the confusion which followed this bomb-shell came a demand that he should produce proof. He did, in the shape of a crumpled and much-thumbed postcard on which the position was stated tersely but unambiguously and signed "Georgi Dimitroff, General Secretary of the Communist International". There was no further room left for doubt as to its authenticity.'[18]

Accounts issued later by the Communist Party suggest that Dutt was the only one to urge the new line before Springhall's return, but that every time he raised it on the Central Committee his supporters 'all ran away'. This seems reasonable enough, as Dutt's weather eye was always sensitive to changes of climate in the Kremlin, and he enjoyed an advantage over the others in his family connections. The same source affirms that Pollitt and Campbell stuck to their former opinion even after Springhall's appearance with the new policy, and were in a minority of two on the final vote.[19] Whether this was the case or no, Pollitt and Campbell were chosen as the scapegoats for the failure to make the change quickly enough. They had been the party's spokesmen who had expressed most clearly the previous policy, making them the obvious choice for writing the two 'self-criticisms'. Campbell's included the following:

> 'With regard to the mistakes which I committed, the Central mistakes were, in my opinion, as follows:
> 1. The Policy of the fight on two fronts, which would have been a correct policy (in peace or in war) with regard to an imperialist Government in alliance with the Soviet Union, was persisted in with regard to a war between two imperialist governments.
> 2. It was persisted in because I narrowed the perspective in such a way as to concentrate on German Fascism as the main enemy of the British working class and failed to see that the way forward for the British, no less than for the German workers, lay in a struggle with the main enemy, i.e. their own imperialists. I thus slipped into a position of national defence in an imperialist war, involving objectively support for our own imperialism. The attitude to the peace proposals followed from this mistaken perspective.
> Undoubtedly the stubborn defence of this wrong position did harm to the Party, when it had to make a sharp turn in a most difficult situation, and I must accept responsibility for resisting what had been proved to be the correct line.'

So Campbell was made to take the blame for the whole of the Popular Front Policy—hardly something into which he alone had accidentally 'slipped'; and he was even made to confess to an opposition to the Stalin/Hitler 'Peace' proposals.

Pollitt's self critique was no more dignified:

> 'After the most serious consideration of the whole situation, I unreservedly accept the policy of the Communist Party and the Communist International, and pledge myself to support it, in explaining, popularizing, and helping to carry it forward to Victory.
> I recognize that my action in resisting the carrying out of the line of the Communist Party and the Communist International represented an impermissible infraction of our Party discipline, and played into the hands of the class enemy, and especially into the hands of the reactionary Labour leaders, who saw in my attitude the justification of their own policy of supporting the Chamberlain Government. I request the Central Committee to accept this declaration and to give me the facilities to prove in deeds that I know how to take my place in the front ranks of our Party in fighting to win the masses for support of the policy of the Communist Party of Great Britain and the

Communist International.'[20]

So while Campbell was made the sacrificial lamb for the Party's previous policy, Pollitt had to take the blame for the patriotism of the Labour leaders who had opposed the Communist Party's own patriotism for years. His statement had all the tones of the confessions of witches, or heretics before the Inquisition—wild, incoherent, and totally out of touch with all reality, past and present.

A wave of disgust spread over the labour movement, whose leaders were to find useful when rejecting overtures for fusion or alliance with the Communist Party in the future. As Herbert Morrison expressed it,

> 'Mr. Pollitt is now more or less dictator of the Communist Party of Great Britain, but I would remind Mr. Pollitt that it was not so long ago Mr. Palme Dutt, a gentleman of another order alto-gether, if I may say so, was the Dictator of Harr Pollitt and the Communist Party. If I mistake not, it was Palme Dutt who ordered and may have dictated the form of humiliating apology that Harry Pollitt and J. R. Campbell had to write because they had supported the War at the beginning, when the Party changed to opposition to the war. Mind you, I rather like Harry Pollitt. I have no violent prejudices against Harry Pollitt as a man, but I say Harry Pollitt went down and down in my estimation when he signed that apology which I do not think he believed. I think it was a lie. And it was done all in the name of Communist discipline. I say that when the Labour Party deals with a political party of that kind, which can order and require men to corrupt their conscience and their real thoughts, it is not a thing that is clean. It is unclean, and if they came into this Labour Party we would become unclean by the very contact we would thereby contract.'[21]

Whatever the humiliation, Pollitt should have counted himself lucky. He was not caught with his trousers on the floor, as his opposite number in France certainly was. The Communist deputies in the Chamber there had voted for the war credits on the 2nd September, and Thorez was among the first to join the army. When the new line came through he had to desert his regiment on the 4th of October, turning up in Moscow a few weeks later. Even the British Communists were caught up in this escapade in an amusing way, when the *Daily Worker* published an interview granted by Thorez to Sam Russell 'somewhere in France'. In some detail the *Daily Worker* described how a guide conducted Russell to him, confidently leading the struggle against the 'Two Hundred Families' who ruled France, in words not unlike a Moscow broadcast. Russell recalled his 'surprise' at being brought face to face with the leader of the French Communists, operating in the underground.

And well he might be surprised. For Thorez was apparently already in Moscow.[22]

Pollitt was luckier: he was not actually called to the boss' office for a ticking off, though he was obliged to resign the secretaryship of the party on October 14th and was sent off to the provinces. He surfaced again as the party's candidate in the Silvertown by-election in the February of the following year.[23]

The relief afforded by these antics was sorely needed, for urgent changes were going on. With a sort of awful inevitability, like the grinding of cogs in some immense machine, the whole party apparatus swung through 180 degrees into the diametrically opposite point of view. 'This war is not a war for democracy against fascism', the *Daily Worker* now assured its readers, 'it is not a war for the defence of peace against aggression.'[24] War to defend English liberties was old hat, for now 'the struggle of the British people against the Chamberlains and Churchills is the best help to the struggle of the Germans against Hitler'.[25] To get this message over, the Party had to go in for a good deal more public confession:

> 'The Communist Party did not immediately judge correctly the complete transformation of the world situation consequent on the defeat by the British and French governments of the aim of the Peace Front and the signing of the Soviet-German Pact.
>
> On September 2nd the Communist Party published a manifesto which presented the aim of the "struggle on two fronts", for the military defeat of Hitler and the political defeat of Chamberlain. This policy was basically incorrect. It failed to take into account the imperialist character of the war and assisted the imperialist camouflage of the war as an "anti-fascist war". The call for the military defeat of Hitler meant objective support for British imperialism and its military victory.'[26]

Apart from making the party unpopular again, the turn brought its own difficulties. Now that they had defined the Second World War as an imperialist war it was reasonable to assume that they would be following Lenin's classic policy of 'revolutionary defeatism', that 'a revolutionary class cannot but wish for the defeat of its government in a reactionary war, cannot fail to see that its military reverses facilitate its overthrow'.[27] The trouble with this was that it had been relegated to the back shelves of Russian policy long ago,

THE SECRET BATTALION

An Examination of the Communist attitude to the Labour Party

Victory THIS Year by William Rust

Defend Socialism— from the Communists.

By TOM TAYLOR
With a Preface by John McNair

Price 1d.

INDEPENDENT LABOUR PARTY
31B, REGENT'S PARK ROAD

HAROLD J. LASKI

TWOPENCE

RAISE HIGH

THE BANNER

By J. GOLLAN

1D.

Labour Youth! Co-operative Youth! Young Communists and Trade Unionists! Together let us write a new page in British Labour History

STALIN'S MEN—

"ABOUT TURN!"

TWOPENCE

THE LABOUR PARTY
Transport House, Smith Square, London, S.W.1

UNITY

TRUE

or

SHAM?

LABOUR PARTY   ONE PENNY

"... this was the political mind of the people who were anxious to support the Labour Party at the last election ..."

Issued by Cardiff Branch Communist Party, 9 St Andrews Cross.

THIS IS NO ORDINARY BY ELECTION. The old Party slogans count for nothing in the present situation.
The need of the moment is :

1. UNITY FOR VICTORY IN 1942
2. JOINT ACTION WITH THE SOVIET UNION.
3. SECOND FRONT IN EUROPE NOW
4. FREEDOM FOR THE INDIAN PEOPLE.

Sir James Grigg might not be a Socialist, but he does want to beat Hitler. Fenner Brockway pretends to be a socialist but his policy means victory for Hitler.

Sir James Grigg is for friendship with the Soviet Union. Fenner Brockway hates the Soviet Union, is against sending war material to the Red Army and competes with Hitler in his lying attacks on Stalin.

Fenner Brockway dare not come out with the real policy of the I.L.P. in this election. When he advocates increased allowances for soldiers and their dependants, he does not explain that the I.L.P. policy would leave us without our great Soviet ally and endanger the lives of our brave lads in the forces.

Fenner Brockway wants freedom for India but does not explain that India can only be free by joining with Britain and Russia in the fight against Fascism. The I.L.P. policy would leave India an easy prey for the Japanese invaders.

What we need is unity   UNITY AGAINST THE COMMON ENEMY. Far better vote for Sir James Grigg.

BROCKWAY OR GRIGG?

HEAR THE COMMUNIST ATTITUDE EXPLAINED

TONIGHT

AT STACEY ROAD SCHOOL AT 7 p.m.

SPEAKERS

IDRIS COX   SOUTH WALES ORGANISER

BETTY BARTLETT   CARDIFF ORGANISER

CARDIFF EAST BY-ELECTION

PUBLISHED BY COMMUNIST PARTY 9 ST ANDREWS CROSS, CARDIFF

Cardiff East, 13th April, 1942.

when Bukharin had declared on Stalin's behalf that in the event of a Russian alliance with a bourgeois state in wartime it was the communists' duty in such a country to assist the alliance to victory.[29]

If Bukharin's reputation was tarnished now by the Trial of the Twenty-One, there were others on hand to answer the disturbing question: 'Is "defeatism" still the best policy for the workers in a capitalist country, associated with the Soviet Union in a war?' 'Obviously not,' replied J. R. Campbell, 'for such a policy (1) would help a fascist victory over the Soviet Union . . . and (2) the overthrow of parliamentary democracy and the extermination of the working class movement.'[29]

But that was written when Campbell was still describing the idea that 'what is developing in the world today is an Imperialist war' as one of the 'commonest and most dangerous fallacies' of 'Trotskyism'.[30]

The assumption that the Soviet Union would (naturally) be allied with the 'democratic' countries in war was not the only thing that would have to be changed in this policy: something resembling Lenin's line of revolutionary defeatism had to be taken back off the shelf and dusted down a bit for front window display. To the same embarrassing question, 'If Germany attacked the Soviet Union, and Britain came in in support of the Soviet Union, would the Communist Party help the Government to carry the war through?' Emil Burns was now obliged to reply that 'whatever government was in office in Britain, the class war would not be suspended, but intensified, precisely in order to defend the Soviet Union and prevent any help being given to fascist Germany'[31] But the degeneration of the Party for the previous ten years prevented its leaders from raising Lenin's slogan without a blush of shame. R. Page Arnot spoke in Glasgow to condemn the ILP for its confusing policy of 'Stop the War' and to contrast it with Lenin's alternative of 'turning the imperialist war into a civil war'. When challenged from the floor on the party's failure to raise that cry, he glibly quoted Lenin again on the dangers of 'the revolutionary phrase'.[32]

Taking his usual rôle when a sharp turn was needed, Palme Dutt supplied the most thorough justification for the party's 'about face' on the issue of the war. His pamphlet *Why This War* defined 'the main world conflict' as being 'between British Imperialism as the principal and most aggressive force of world reaction, and world Socialism, led by the Soviet Union'. Those naive enough to think that Germany as well might have something to do with it were told that 'if Peace is refused, it is plain to all in the present conditions that the responsibility of continuing the war will lie with the British and French ruling classes'.[33] This was a direct echo of the Joint

Declaration of the Soviet and German Governments after the fall of Poland, which affirmed that 'if, however, these efforts of both governments remain unsuccessful, it will be established thereby that England and France bear the responsibility for the continuation of the war'.

By laying all the blame for the continuation of the war on the shoulders of the British government, Dutt had converted the Communist Party into an instrument of Hitler's propaganda in this country. Readers of the *Daily Worker* were exhorted to defy the blackout by turning on the lights, and Hitler's conquest of the low countries came out in its pages as 'Britain spreads the war to Holland'.[34]

Dutt himself did not have to carry the can for this policy, but countless ordinary members did, bravely standing by what they believed to be the cause of Communism and the working class in its hour of trial. Teachers in the party even had to enter their classrooms greeted by the pupils with a mock Nazi salute.[35]

Dutt pressed his point in yet another pamphlet entitled *We Fight for Life*, where he attempted to spread the blame a little more evenly:

'This war is a continuation of the war of 1914-18, as Churchill himself said. It continues the war of Anglo-American imperialism. There are the same false slogans of "liberty" and "justice" and "the rights of small nations". There are the same aims of the imperialists to win the spoils of world domination, to maintain and extend their power, to save capitalism . . . Two world blocs of robber powers are fighting in this war of world domination.'[36]

Dutt certainly had a thick skin. On November 14th 1939 he went so far as to say that the Labour Party had 'signed its death-warrant' by its 'whole-hearted participation in the blood-stained crime of this war'. Others were quick to point out that before the war the Communists themselves 'were the chief war-mongers and share joint responsibility with the Labour leaders for the deception and betrayal of the working-class movement into the blood-stained crime of this war'.[37]

Now the line was clear again the party had the go-ahead to work over details of the new policy. Commander Edgar Young was taken with 'horror' at the prospect of coming to the end of the war 'whether victorious or not' under the leadership of those 'who are now imposing upon us a regime which becomes increasingly like that which we are *supposed to be* fighting'.[38] Sam Blackwell lambasted the government for the lack of ARP facilities, which proved that there must be a government of the people that will build bomb-proof shelters',[39] whilst James Johnson produced a 'Startling Exposure of the Financial Interests who are Exploiting the War'.[40] The war was two months old before an official statement finally got round to describing what had been going on from the first day: 'a heyday for bullying foremen and managers', who have 'tried it on, who have sacked men and women indiscriminately, who have told men "work later tonight" '[41]

The party lurched leftwards, to lend some credibility to the new turn. When Labour took the step of entering government they were told that 'a real Labour Opposition could bring the Government tumbling down and send a peace call which would echo through all the warring countries'.[42] As a party manifesto issued then expressed it,

'To their eternal shame the Labour Party leaders have offered to enter a new "National Government" in combination with the most ruthless jingo representatives of capitalism. These same leaders who maintained Chamberlain in power now accept the leadership of Churchill and come to the rescue of the Diehard Imperialists in the intensification of the war . . .

For them (i.e. the capitalists) the war is no anti-fascist war, but an imperialist war, a war against the German people to inflict a new super Versailles, a war on the working class in all countries and against the Socialist Soviet Union.

End the political truce. End the policy of unity with capitalism and war. Fight for the cause of the most oppressed peoples—the colonial peoples of the British Empire. Proclaim unity with the Socialist Soviet Union. Let our aim be the victory of working class power and of Socialism . . . against all the attacks of reaction let the workers' battle cry resound anew: "Workers of all lands, unite!"'[43]

It was a stirring call, but it might have carried a little more conviction if those making it had not spent the last three years condemning that sort of thing as 'counter-revolutionary Trotskyism'. For by now the party itself was trying to be as 'left' as possible: when Attlee and the other Labour leaders agreed to enter the cabinet first and consult the Labour Party afterwards, the party described it as 'the measure of advance already made towards fascist forms, towards National Socialist methods in the Labour Party'.[44] So after ten years, momentous years of change and conflict, the party had come round full circle, back to the language of the 'Third Period'.

While the Communists appeared to have learned nothing, the

Labour leaders had learned a trick or two. Communism, Attlee explained to a conference of Labour and trades union delegates, was 'in its methods of repression, brutality and dictatorship' 'only too like Nazism. The Communists have no right to the name of Socialists or Communists. They are Stalinites'.[45] Even *Tribune* stopped printing Stalin's speeches and articles.

The party press in the meantime, was going from absurdity to absurdity. 'Red Army Takes Bread to Starving Peasants' was its description of Stalin's conquest of Eastern Poland,[46] otherwise defined as 'the extension of Socialist liberation for the 13 millions of Western Ukraine and Western Byelorussia'.[47] The Winter War came out as 'Behind the Red Army Life Begins for the Finnish People'.[48] There was not a great deal of outcry when Herbert Morrison used the powers accorded him under Defence Regulation 2D to ban the *Daily Worker* (January 21st, 1941) though the Party itself was never banned, as its French counterpart was.

There was no need. Its showing during by-elections (where it operated under a variety of fronts such as 'the Workers' and Pensioners' Anti-War', and 'Labour Stop the War') was derisory, except when its candidates gave the workers a chance to break the electoral truce by putting in an anti-Tory vote.[49] Its greatest success in the trade union movement was a resolution condemning the war, that went through the annual conference of the Shop Assistants' Union in March 1940, though even here it had been proposed by a Trotskyist and only got through with the backing of a bloc of traditional pacifist supporters. For a resolution endorsing the foreign policy of the Soviet Union put up at the same time was resoundingly defeated.[50]

Opportunities certainly existed for the Communist Party to place itself at the head of the rising tide of working class anti-war opinion, but it forfeited them by its equivocation. It still refused to call for revolutionary defeatism, or for the dictatorship of the proletariat. It certainly did not make Lenin's distinction[51] between the pacifist sentiments of the masses and the cynical misuse of them by others. 'To talk of war to the end', said the *Daily Worker* on the 30th September, 1939, 'which means the wholesale slaughter of the youth of Europe, would be sheer madness', skating over the possibilities for turning the imperialist war into a civil war. A reformist veneer was placed over any expression of popular resentment against the hardships of war, such as when the London Communists tried to divert the demand for air raid facilities on a par with those of the better classes into a petition addressed to 'the Right Hon. Winston Churchill, MP, PC.'[52]

In the same fashion, it refused to raise the answer of workers' revolution as the only guarantee against a robber peace and the recurrence of further wars. It fell back instead on its old Popular Front illusions, such as when Dutt assured everyone that 'if a People's Government came to power in this country, it would immediately make its proposals for peace to all governments and all peoples'.[53] So now we got the contradictory position of holding a People's Front and a Social Fascist policy at one and the same time!

The failure of the Communist Party to carry out any of Lenin's policy on war was due to the fundamental change that had come over it during the period of the Popular Front, when it had recruited so many of the pacifist middle class elements who were now deserting it so rapidly. For all the weight of its propaganda was thrown, not behind the concept of a workers' dictatorship, but behind that of a 'Peoples' Government' whose class character was deliberately left undefined. They were even behind some of the Labour leaders, who could still take time off from prosecuting imperialist war inside a bourgeois cabinet, to claim that 'we can only win this war by the Socialist transformation of Great Britain'.[54]

The New Popular Front campaign got off the ground with the foundation of a 'People's Vigilance Committee' in Holborn Town Hall on the 7th July, 1940. It issued a manifesto entitled *A Call to the People* written by D. N. Pritt, who had just been slung out of the Labour Party for supporting Stalin's attack on Finland and writing the book *Must War Spread?*[55] It was to organise a 'People's Convention', which brought together some 2,234 delegates on January 12th, 1941, to hear Pritt describe how the government was 'moving steadily all along the line towards a general compulsory system of a fascist pattern'. The six-point programme still carefully avoided proletarian dictatorship, or the necessity for turning the imperialist war into a civil war:

'(1) Defence of the People's Living Standards.
(2) Defence of the People's Democratic and Trade Union rights.
(3) Adequate air-raid precautions, deep bomb-proof shelters, rehousing and relief of victims.
(4) Friendship with the Soviet Union.
(5) A People's Government truly representative of the whole people and able to inspire the confidence of the working people of the world.
(6) A people's Peace that gets rid of the causes of war.'[56]

There was no need to pick holes in this list, as it was threadbare already. Only a workers' government, not one representing 'the whole people' (the National Government claimed to be that) could inspire trust in the international working class, and only a revolution that placed it there could deal such a blow against imperialism as to remove the causes of future wars. The strange absence of classes among the 'people' who made up this front organisation even raised comment at the time. In any case, if this gathering was meant to be representative of them, the people had rather more than their usual share of publicists, professional lawyers, clerics and dance band conductors. It was all plainly inspired by a nostalgic glance back at the thirties, when classes all disappeared in a welter of 'progressives' who supported the Soviet Union in the pursuit of 'peace'.

Not that the Convention had much credibility. *Tribune* noted with some amusement that the standing orders committee not only chose all the speakers and saw that their speeches were all roneoed, but that the press received them in some cases before they were even delivered! ('Ananias also Ran', *Tribune*, 17th January, 1941, pp.10-11.)

Nine days afterwards the government put a ban on the *Daily Worker*, a serious inroad into democratic rights and the freedom of the workers' press. Five months later the German invasion of the Soviet Union brought to an end this phase of the Communist Party's life, and opened up another.

Footnotes

1 Estimated annual rearmament expenditure, 1936-9:
   1936   £60.7 million
   1937   £104.2 million
   1938   £182.2 million
   1939   £273.1 million
2 The aircraft production figures speak for themselves:
   1938   240 a month
   1939   660 a month
3 ARP expenditure shows the character of the coming war to an even greater degree.
   1938   £9.5 million
   1939   £51   million
4 A. J. P. Taylor, *English History 1914-1945*, Oxford, 1965, p.491.
5 Fortunately, this was never actually implemented, to the knowledge of the authors.
6 A. J. P. Taylor, *op. cit*, p. 493.

7 Lenin (and Zinoviev), *Socialism and War*, Peking Edition, November 1966, p. 17.
8 Lenin, *op. cit*, pp. 43-4.
9 J. R. Campbell, *Question and Answers on Communism*, CPGB.
10 *Daily Worker*, 23rd August, 1939.
11 Draft Programme to be Submitted to the 16th Party Congress, October 1939, dated 29th August, 1939, p. 32.
12 'Protests to Labour: Joins Communists', in the *Daily Worker*, 31st August, 1939.
13 *Daily Worker*, 2nd September, 1939.
14 *Challenge*, 2nd September, 1939.
15 *Daily Worker*, 4th September, 1939.
16 H. Pollitt, *How to Win the War*, CPGB pamphlet, 14th September, 1939.
17 *Challenge*, 23rd September, 1939.
18 D. Hyde, *I Believed*, London, 1952, p. 70. Presumably this message (or whatever it was), contained the gist of the pamphlet later to be published by the Party, Dimitroff's *Communism and the War* (including the ECCI Manifesto of November 6th, 1939).
19 M. Johnstone, 'What Kind of Communist Party History?', in *Our History* (journal of the history group of the CPGB), no. 4, February, 1979.
20 J. R. Campbell and H. Pollitt, Declarations of 19th November, 1939, in *World News and Views*, vol. xix, no. 56, 2nd December, 1939, pp. 1118ff. *Cf. Daily Worker*, 16th February, 1940.
21 Herbert Morrison, Speech on Communist Affiliation to the 42nd Annual Conference of the Labour Party, London, 1943—Official Report, p. 167.
22 'Outlawed French Leader Tells Why He is Hunted', in the *Daily Worker*, 4th November, 1939, *cf.* H. M. Wicks, *Eclipse of October*, London, 1958, pp. 375-6.
23 *Daily Worker*, 16th and 21st February, 1940.
24 Manifesto published by the *Daily Worker*, 7th October, 1939.
25 *World News and Views*, vol. xix, pp. 1015f.
26 'The Outbreak of War', in *The Communist Party in War Time*, (a record of activities and documents issued up to March 15th, 1940). CPGB, pp. 3-4.
27 Lenin (and Zinoviev), *Socialism and War*, Peking Edition, November, 1966, p. 25.
28 J. Braunthal, *History of the International*, London, 1967, vol. ii, pp. 258-9.
29 J. R. Campbell, *Questions and Answers on Communism*, CPGB pamphlet, March, 1938.
30 J. R. Campbell, 'The Trotskyist Danger', in *For Peace and Plenty*, Report of the 15th Congress of the CPGB, September, 1938, p. 95.
31 Emil Burns, 'Difficulties Facing Peace', CPGB pamphlet (n.d.).
32 'CP Sits on the Fence', in *Workers' Diary* no. 93, 1st February, 1940.
33 R. Palme Dutt, *Why This War?*, CPGB pamphlet, November, 1939.
34 The *Daily Worker* of May 11th, 1940, published without comment the German memorandum justifying the invasion of the low countries. *Cf.* the comment passed by the 41st annual conference of the Labour Party, Westminster, May, 1942—Official Report, p. 159, and *Communists in War: How the Communists Played Hitler's Game when Britain was in Peril*, Labour Party duplicated pamphlet, June, 1945. Britain had earlier also received all the blame for the extension of the war to Norway and Denmark in an *Izvestia* report reprinted in the *Daily Worker* of the 12th April, 1940.
35 'The Events of 1939-41 and the Communist Party', Symposium of the CP History Group, 21st April, 1979.
36 R. Palme Dutt, *We Fight For Life*, CPGB pamphlet, pp. 5-7.
37 *Daily Worker*, 14th November, 1939, *cf. Workers' Diary*, vol. i, no. 26, 14th November, 1939.
38 Commander Edgar Young, *A People's Peace* (emphasis in original), CPGB

pamphlet.
39 Sam Blackwell, *Coventry—What Next?* CPGB pamphlet.
40 James Johnson, *The Men Behind the War*, CPGB pamphlet.
41 *The War and the Workers*, CPGB pamphlet, 1st November, 1939.
42 'The Government Crisis', Editorial in the *Daily Worker*, 6th May, 1940.
43 Political Bureau Statement on the War and the Government Crisis, in the *Daily Worker*, 11th May, 1940.
44 'Communist Appeal to Delegates (at the Bournemouth Labour Party Conference), in the *Daily Worker*, 13th May, 1940.
45 'Mr Attlee Attacks Communists', in the *Daily Worker*, 15th January, 1940.
46 *Daily Worker*, 20th September, 1939.
47 'The Outbreak of War', in *The Communist Party in War Time*, the Record of Activities and Documents issued up to March 15th, 1940. CPGB, pp. 4-5.
48 *Daily Worker*, 2nd January, 1940.
49 Harry Pollitt gained only 966 votes against Labour at Silvertown on a CP platform in February 1940, and 'Labour Stop the War' took only 791 votes at Battersea against Labour (April, 1940), and 2,401 at Pollock against a National Government candidate (May, 1940). But the 'Workers' and Pensioners' Anti-War' candidate reaped no less than 6,616 for the Tory's 17,914 at Kettering in March 1940, a respectable result, given the atmosphere of the time.
50 *Daily Worker*, 26th March, 1940: Margaret Johns, interview with Al·Richardson, 4th February, 1978.
51 Above, p. 61.
52 Undated petition put out by the London District of the CPGB.
53 R. Palme Dutte, *We Fight for Life*, CPGB pamphlet (undated), p. 22.
54 Laski, Speech to the 40th Annual Conference of the Labour Party, Westminster, June, 1941—Official Report, p. 129.
55 D. N. Pritt, *A Call to the People: A Manifesto of the People's Vigilance Committee*.
56 *Cf.* Hugo Dewar, *Communist Politics in Britain*, London, 1976, pp. 136-7.

Chapter Five

Trooping the Colour: The Communists in Politics, 1941-5

At dawn on June 22nd, 1941, Hitler's artillery barrage opened up along the border shared by the USSR and Germany in Poland, and his tanks crossed the line and began to penetrate the Russian defences.

Churchill had tried to warn Stalin about this, without much success, and offered him an immediate alliance, while comparing him to the Devil and admitting that 'no one has been a more persistent opponent of Communism than I have been'.[1] An Anglo-Soviet Mutual Aid Pact was signed on July 12th, followed by a more comprehensive agreement, including a plan for a Second Front, in the following May. Stalin's honeymoon with the Western powers was sealed by the dissolution of the Comintern on July 23rd, 1943, which served as an hors d'oeuvre to a carve-up of the world at a meeting of the superpowers in Teheran in November. The rearrangement of Eastern Europe was settled in the same amicable atmosphere in the 'Percentages Agreement' made in Moscow between Churchill and Stalin in October, 1944, and when victory was finally in sight this principle of horse-trading the fate of nations was maintained in the Yalta Accords of February 1945.

What was the rôle reserved for the British Communist Party in these world-shattering events?

Again, when the curtain rose on the new scene, this actor was not on stage, for he had not been given his new lines. The Party's enthusiasm for democratic war against Nazism had cooled in the realisation that the conflict was, after all, an imperialist one. It had been assumed once more that a twist of Soviet Policy had become a permanent part of the World Communist Outlook. A statement reproduced from *Izvestia* in the *Daily Worker* had assured British readers that:

'For a number of months before the Pact (i.e. Molotov/ Ribbentrop) Britain and France made persistent attempts to harness the Soviet Union in their chariot, to use the Soviet Union for their imperialist aims. Above all they strove to provoke armed conflict between the USSR and Germany . . .'

The good neighbourly and friendly relations between the Soviet Union and Germany was not based on fortuitous considerations of a transient nature, but on the fundamental state interests of both the USSR and Germany. This truth has long been understood in the USSR and Germany'.[2]

So while the world hummed with rumours of a conflict soon to include the Soviet Union, a week before it happened the YCL newspaper was asking the question: 'Why has Ambrose's band been taken off the air?', a 'question thousands of dance and swing enthusiasts will want answered'.[3] D. N. Pritt's 'alternative' to the Churchill government was still 'for the working class to end the policy of coalition and to take the leading rôle in building a powerful independent opposition'.[4] A month after the attack E. M. Winterton continued to describe the Labour Party Conference (accurately enough) as meeting 'under Tory patronage', while Dutt was looking forward to Hitler's defeat 'if the working class organisations fulfil their responsibility of leadership and break with the policies of coalition with Tory reaction'.[5]

Then doing a quick double to get in step, Pollitt announced the change of line, affirming that 'in supporting the Churchill government we do it wholeheartedly and without reservations',[6] with Dutt eating humble pie a month afterwards offering 'the most wholehearted support to the Churchill government in every measure it adopts'.[7] It was all the more galling for Dutt, as he had been the main architect of the previous change from this very policy in the Autumn of 1939. His report, adopted with the same unanimity as the new position, had stated that

'Only the international working class can end the war. By defeating our own imperialists and winning the victory for the forces of the working class and of the people in Britain, we hasten the conditions for the ending of the war.'[8]

Enthusiasm was expressed for the new view. 'A fight for a united national front', affirmed Pollitt, 'means support for Churchill's government and all measures for a common victory'.[9] Communists even had some 'measures' to suggest for themselves:

'Mobilise every able-bodied man and woman for war service in the armed forces, civil defence and industry. No evasions to be tolerated. Speed the training and placing of women in all industries to release large numbers of men for the armed forces.'[10]

A whole reversal of language and philosophy had to take place again, and the world 'turned upside down'. People as well as policies changed into their opposites. Sikorski, a 'semi-Fascist', De Gaulle, a 'petty adventurer' and a 'discredited puppet', and Metaxas, 'originally pro-Hitler' became 'our gallant allies'. Churchill, formerly quoted to the effect that 'I will not pretend that, if I had to choose between Communism and Nazism, I would choose Communism', [11] was now quoted as:

'Two years ago the Prime Minister, in the critical days of Dunkirk, made a speech which found an echo in the hearts of every lad and girl: "We will fight on the beaches. We will fight in the hills. . ."[12]

What they had been saying about him at the time was something different from this, such as "Let the Labour Leaders fawn on him as they will. The rank and file of the Labour movement do not trust this man".'[13]

Such a change at the crisis point of a world war could not fail to raise comment within the Labour movement. But proud of the shortness of their own memories, Communist leaders could only 'notice with some little interest the various sneers and scoffings about the Communist Party changing its line once again',[14] in which they professed to see only 'small matters, interesting only to narrow minds'.[15] Included among these 'narrow minds' were the National Council of Labour, the TUC and the NEC of the Labour Party, who took it as yet another piece of evidence that the 'Communist Party during the war has thus again demonstrated its irresponsible and unstable character',[16] describing its antics as 'political somersaulting of the most contemptible kind'.[17] Ordinary supporters were scandalised by the eagerness with which the Communists embraced their Tory allies. 'I do not like to associate with the Tories', said a South Wales Councillor to the Labour Party Conference, 'but Harry Pollitt does.'[18]

The policy switchround went from the top circles of government and parliament right down to the industrial labourer and the army private. A directive went out to Communists in the army to make adjustments   in   their   conduct,   described   by   an   eye-witness:

'Of course at this time you must remember that the Stalinists were very friendly towards me and one or two people who were pals of mine—you know, who I'd influenced, because the Stalinists at that time were against the war. You see, this was the time following the Stalin/Hitler pact, and for a time everything in the garden was rosy—you know what I mean, they used to agree with me wholeheartedly, but in 1941 after Hitler attacked Stalin, it was amazing! Because all these fellows like myself (none of us were in the slightest what the authorities would call "good soldiers": I mean, we were always in trouble and all the rest of it)—these Stalinists were the same. They weren't interested in the war at all! But directly Stalin came into the war—well, they turned into the best soldiers! In fact, one of them told me that that was the directive—'You must be the best soldiers in the army. Everybody must look up to you and respect you'. It was quite a turnabout, believe me!

But it had its funny side, because in the army, you know, it's the old saying "Give a dog a bad name". Well, once you've "got a bad name" it takes a long time to live down. Well, some of these Stalinists had very bad names . . .I remember . . . Laurie Jones. He joined up the very same day with me in my company, and he was always in trouble. Well then, of course—as I say—suddenly the directive came through that they should be good soldiers and I think that for the first time since he joined the army, Laurie Jones cleaned his boots, and cleaned his webbing, and all this kind of stuff. People couldn't believe it was the same bloke! It was very, very funny!'[19]

Political memories are short, but not as short as all that. It was necessary for the Communist Party to go overboard with the new policy to convince 'certain elements who know no better' who continued to 'accuse the Communist Party of impeding the national effort as far as production is concerned'.[20] As Pollitt recognised in his letter to CP members announcing the new line, 'it is necessary to avoid giving any impression that our present policy is determined solely because the Soviet Union has been attacked' (*For the Defeat of Fascism—An Appeal to our Party*). The Party members were obliged to outdo the rest of the Labour movement, even cabinet ministers, in their patriotism and dedication to the national interest. A series of pamphlets appeared in the fetching colour scheme of red, white and blue.[21] The Peace Pledge Union was accused by Claude Cockburn of

Daily Worker

No. 3006 — REGISTERED AT THE G.P.O. AS A NEWSPAPER — One Penny

SATURDAY, SEPTEMBER 2, 1939

FINAL EDITION

THE THREE THOUSANDTH number of the DAILY WORKER is issued today. At this vital moment support for the paper is bigger than ever in its history. Circulation has reached record heights. Contributions to the Fighting Fund have never been more generous. AND THE NECESSITY FOR THE PAPER HAS NEVER BEEN GREATER.

With this three thousandth number make new efforts to help your paper, help to create even better records. You can do no better work.

WE RELY ON YOU.

NAZIS PLUNGE WORLD INTO WAR

Poland Invaded and Towns Bombed

CONSCRIPTION FROM 18-41 IN BRITAIN

THE MAD DOGS OF EUROPE—HITLER AND HIS NAZI GOVERNMENT—HAVE SET OUT ON THEIR LAST BLOODY ADVENTURE.

IN THE GREY HOURS OF YESTERDAY MORNING, GERMAN BOMBERS SWOOPING OVER THE POLISH CITIES OF CRACOW, KATTOWITZ, AND WARSAW ITSELF, HURLED THEIR BOMBS UPON THE PACKED TENEMENTS.

THE POLISH GOVERNMENT APPEALED TO THE BRITISH GOVERNMENT TO STAND BY ITS PLEDGE TO POLAND.

The British and French Governments did not act immediately. Instead, the Prime Minister in the House of Commons, declared that unless the German Government were to call an immediate halt to its aggression, the British Ambassador would be withdrawn from Berlin.

While bombs rained upon the Polish towns, the British and French Governments were seemingly still delayed to give an immediate answer to this act of brutal aggression.

IN THE HOUSE OF COMMONS LAST NIGHT WAS PASSED POWERING THE GOVERNMENT TO CONSCRIPT...

THE REAL NEWS

The people of Britain at this time want facts, all the facts. They want also they can trust. They want the Daily Worker. New thousands are turning to the paper every day.

To enable the Daily Worker to continue publication, readers old and new, rich and poor, have sent us forward with their sixpences, and shillings, their ten pounds and fifty pounds. The record sum of

£1629

SOLIDARITY PROGRAMME

Daily Worker

No. 3158 — REGISTERED AT THE G.P.O. AS A NEWSPAPER — One Penny

TUESDAY, APRIL 9, 1940

NORWAY ACCUSES ALLIES

'Most Unwarranted Violation Of Neutrality'

DEMANDS IMMEDIATE REMOVAL OF MINES AND WARSHIPS

THE POSSIBILITY OF A HUGE EXTENSION OF THE WAR LOOMED UP OVER EUROPE YESTERDAY, AS THE BRITISH AND FRENCH GOVERNMENTS ANNOUNCED THAT DURING THE PREVIOUS NIGHT THEY HAD ORDERED THEIR WARSHIPS TO INVADE THE NEUTRAL WATERS OF NORWAY AND LAY THREE MINEFIELDS THERE.

Instant and bitter protest came from the Norwegian Government.

"THE NORWEGIAN GOVERNMENT," SAYS THE OFFICIAL COMMUNIQUE ISSUED IN OSLO YESTERDAY MORNING PROTESTS STRONGLY AGAINST THIS "MOST SEVERE AND MOST UNWARRANTED VIOLATION OF NEUTRALITY SINCE THE WAR STARTED.

"Norway demands that the mines be removed immediately and that Allied warships guarding the mines shall be removed.

"The Norwegian Government reserves the right to take any...

Daily Worker

No. 3054 — REGISTERED AT THE G.P.O. AS A NEWSPAPER — One Penny

SATURDAY, NOVEMBER 4, 1939

OUTLAWED FRENCH LEADER TELLS WHY HE IS HUNTED

HERE IS THE BIGGEST STORY THAT HAS COME TO ANY NEWSPAPER FROM "SOMEWHERE IN FRANCE" SINCE THE WAR BEGAN.

THE OFFICIAL "WAR CORRESPONDENTS" DAILY DESPATCH THEIR STORIES OF CONDUCTED TOURS ALONG THE BATTLE LINES OF THE NEW IMPERIALIST WAR.

They tell what they are allowed to tell of the working men "digging in" before the slaughter starts.

Of what is really happening in France, of what the people of France are thinking and doing, not a word has been published.

Not a word on the work of the 4,000,000 trade unionists, or the 300,000 members of the Communist Party, declared illegal and persecuted by the Daladier Government.

Interviewed— Interviewer

MAURICE THOREZ, general secretary of the French Communist Party, is hunted by the French authorities. Along with a few other Communist Deputies he avoided arrest when police swooped on Communist leaders shortly after the outbreak of war and is carrying on his work illegally.

Sam Russell was Daily Worker correspondent in Paris. He was Daily Worker correspondent in Spain in the closing days of the war. He was the last war appear correspondent to leave the Catalonian front.

". . . in this way the aggressor powers are the fascist powers, Germany, Italy and Japan . . ."

Daily Worker

No. 2024

REGISTERED AT THE G.P.O. AS A NEWSPAPER   One Pe y

SATURDAY, SEPTEMBER 30, 19.9   FINAL EDITION

" Communism has become a power and strength in France which no imperialist Government can destroy; the Fren · proletariat, firmly imbued with the great teachings of Lenin and Stalin, will find the ways and means of affording protection for its Communist Party, will fight tenaciously against those who seek to attempt to destroy it, and will follow its leader to eventual triumph a :: all its enemies, and will bring peace to a free, strong and happy France.

" The Communist Party of Great Britain calls upon the British workers, and all organisations, to voice its strong condemnation of the oppression, and vigorously to protest to the French Embassy."

(See Page Three)

PEACE OFFER TO EUROPE

Soviet-German Declaration On War In West

NEW EASTERN FRONTIERS FIXED

A N OFFER OF IMMEDIATE PEACE TO THE WESTER.V WORLD —ON THE BASIS OF THE PEACE ALREADY ESTABLISHED IN EAST EUROPE—WAS MAD. YESTERDAY BY THE GOVERN-MENT OF THE UNION OF SOCIALIST SOVIET REPUBLICS.

W..h this offer, t e German Gover: nent associated itself.

In a ;int communiqué the two Governments yesterda, declareu that:—

" The German Government and the Government of the U.S.S.R. naving, by a Treaty signed today, finally settled the questions arising from the dissolution of the Polish State, and thereby created a firm foundation for a lasting peace in Eastern Europe, they in mutual agreement express the opinion that the liquidation of the present ar between Germany o the one hand and Great Britain and France on the other would meet the interests of all nations.

" Therefore both Governments will direct their common efforts, if necessary in accord with other friendly Powers, in order to attain this aim as early as possible

" If however these efforts of both Governments remain futile, it will thereby be established that Great Britain and France bear the responsibility for the continuation of the war, and in case of a continuation of the war, the Governments of Germany and the U.S.S.R. will consult each other regarding necessary measures

British Capitalist

The Daily Worker says...

A PEOPLE'S GOVERNMENT COULD SECURE LASTING PEACE

RISING from the wreck of Nazi aggres-·-- ···· in Mos----tion because of the way ···

ALL QUIET IN THE WEST—WHY?

Daily Worker

No. 3015

REGISTERED AT THE G.P.O. AS A NEWSPAPER

WEDNESDAY, SEPTEMBER 20, 1939

One Penny

FIRST EDITION

Daily Wor

No. 2108

REGISTERED AT THE G.P.O. AS A NEWSPAPER

One Penny

WEDNESDAY, JANUARY 3, 1940

BEHIND THE RED ARMY LIFE BEGINS FOR FINNISH PEOPLE

Eyewitness Story

F IRST, AS USUAL, WITH THE REAL NEWS, THE DAILY WORKER IS PROUD TO BE ABLE TO GIVE ITS READERS TODAY THIS EYEWITNESS ACCOUNT REACHING THE BRITISH P..BLIC OF WHAT IS REALLY HAPPENING IM-MEDIATELY BEHIND THE LINES IN FINLAND AS THE RED ARMY BATTLES FOR THE LIBERATION OF THE FINNISH WORKING PEOPLE FROM THE WHITE GUARDS.

Reporter Levitin's straightforward story of events immediately following the Red advance in the south central sector of the front offers a vivid contrast to the tales being manufactured in the White Guard propagandist agencies at Helsinki.

Here, for the first time, is the real story of the working men and women supposed to be "united" behind Field-Marshal Baron von Mannerheim. And here, in the words of one of the Red Army Commanders to a Finnish peasant woman, is the real :aning for the Finnish people of the coming of the Red Army.

" Why die? Real life is only just beginning."

From MICHAEL LEVITIN

With the Red Army on the Central Front

FINNISH officers are forcing the peasants ... ...

RED ARMY TAKES BREAD TO STARVING PEASANTS

G REETED EVERYWHERE BY THE CHEERS OF THE WORKING POPULATION, THE RED ARMY YESTERDAY CONTINUE) ITS ADVANCE INTO BYELO-RUSSIA AND THE UKRAINE.

Meanwh it was confirmed that Marshal Smigly-Rydz, commander-in-chief of the Polish army, is at Cernauti, Rumania, with members of the Polish Government.

On the Western Front a ! reported that " a restricted enen

A Frie·
Hi·
Comen

THE Han. Dolly '···· ···· ···

Busmen Will Not

acting 'on lines closely parallelling those of Nazi policy',[22] and other opponents of the war became 'Fascists in disguise'.[23] As for the rest of the movement, it was castigated for the 'easy-going Liberalism' and 'dangerous toleration' extended to dissidents, and a high moral tone was adopted in demands for 'No Mercy to Traitors'.[24]

Patriotism crowded into the pages of the newly-legalised *Daily Worker*. D-Day was described as 'a People's Invasion' accompanied by photographs of Eisenhower, Montgomery and Tedder over the caption 'They lead us into battle'.[25] Occasionally the Communists showed that they were aware which was the senior partner in the alliance, by changing their British patriotism into American, such as when they chided the House of Commons over its suspicion towards the monetary conference called by President Roosevelt:

> 'The Lords debate will, we hope, show an advance on that of the House of Commons, which was overcharged with fear and sus- picion of the USA.
>   Without the wholehearted co-operation of the USA it will be impossible to build an international organisation for the main- tenance of peace. If the monetary conference called by President Roosevelt fails, the whole structure of Anglo-American co- operation will be endangered.'[26]

Not that they were uncritical supporters of the operations of American imperialism. When quiet descended on the Western Front for a weekend, they complained that it was 'incredible that hostilities were held up' whilst 'American chaplains read the religious services within hearing of the German front line and wished the Germans a happy Easter'.[27]

Their own sentiments went beyond wishing the Germans the compliments of the season. The whole of the German people— Hitler's first victims—was charged with some sort of original sin. 'Millions of the youth behave worse than beasts', wrote William Rust, 'and the entire nation must take responsibility for crimes committed in its name.'[28] Soviet demands for the stiffest reparations and the most extreme punitive measures found justification in 'the corruption of a whole people'. Allied soldiers were warned that fraternisation would mean contamination with the 'moral peril' of a nation which did not manifest 'the slightest general understanding of guilt for the crimes in which it has taken an active part, in which it shares responsibility'.[29] When ILP member Walter Padley, representing NUDAW, described the language of the TUC Report of 1944 which held the German people alone responsible for the war

as 'a surrender to all that Lord Vansittart was preaching', Frank
Foulkes of the ETU answered:

> 'The argument for allowing the German people to disregard their
> responsibilities for this war reminded him of the argument of the
> 'poor   widow'   used   by   Railway   Directors   whenever
> nationalisation of railways was under discussion. There were very
> few poor widows and there were very few people in Germany
> outside the concentration camps who had put up any fight against
> the   Nazi   regime.   Individuals   who   had   stayed   outside
> concentration camps in Nazi Germany must be made to prove
> that they were not responsible.' (TUC Conference Report, 1944,
> p. 256.)

Disgust rose among socialists over this racism; the ILP had long
opposed it, especially in Douglas Brown's pamphlet *Commonsense
versus Vansittartism* (October, 1943), and sections of the mainstream
of the Labour movement were horrified. Laski contributed a
brochure of his own to the problem, *Are the Germans Really Human?*
(Left Book Club, 1941), and even the saner wing of the
Conservatives could see that 'war guilt' and reparations imposed on
Germany after the First World War had been a substantial cause of
the Second.

The details of how these right wing views were spread round the
movement have been too well dealt with by others to make it
necessary to repeat them here,[30] though we might add that the
Communists were obliged to repeat them all the more because their
own pro-German propaganda before 1941 was still fresh in people's
memories. Moreover, Fleet Street took some time to understand the
Party's change of line, and when strikes broke out, like a stuck
gramophone record, the media continued to blame the Communists
for them. On other occasions uncomfortable reminders came to the
surface to suggest that the long-term interests of 'the Democratic
Allies' might not be forever compatible, such as when former
Comintern agent David Springhall was convicted for spying on
behalf of 'a foreign power'. The Party was obliged to expel him on
the spot, as well as having to issue a statement that

> 'The CP will welcome and give the fullest facilities for any invest-
> igation in regard to the baseless allegations that it is being used for
> any purpose detrimental to the national interests.'[31]

For the Party's dedication to national unity (or rather the Stalin-
Churchill-Roosevelt Pact) was sincere. 'If however any putting

forward of impossible demands is permitted', wrote Harry Pollitt, 'any irresponsible fighting of by-elections in present conditions, then our party simply plays into the hands of the dark forces who are waiting for such an opportunity to take advantage of dissension and splits in the national fight against Fascism'.[32] It meant that the Communists had now entered the wartime no-contest pact of the other parties, as well as throwing the whole of their weight against the 'impossible demands' of the shop floor.

Already by the 6th July they had withdrawn their candidate in the Greenock by-election, which they had (apparently) a chance of winning, in order to avoid 'misunderstanding'; and they were not only anxious not to challenge the government themselves, but even more to prevent anyone else from having any opportunity to show their dissatisfaction with the ruling class on an electoral level.

Their new policy here was very much swimming against the tide of opinion now turning in the movement. As war went on, feeling inside the Labour Party against the no-contest pact with the Tories was held down with increasing difficulty. With the narrowest of margins, 66,000 votes, the executive only just managed to defeat an amendment to end the electoral truce at the annual Labour Party conference of May, 1942.[33] The ILP vote consistently increased, and the Party took on a new lease of life; and when Sir Richard Acland's 'Common Wealth' Party gave the workers a chance to express an anti-Tory vote, the government's nominees went down to defeat on three occasions. A by-election at Bilston was won by the government by a majority of only 400, and the Tory candidate, Lieutenant Colonel W. E. Gibbons, openly admitted that 'it is clear that the majority of the Labour Party in the division voted for my ILP opponent'.[34]

The Communists were not so much oblivious to this feeling as consciously against it. When the ILP contested a Tory seat at a by-election in Edinburgh in December, 1941, the local CP branch distributed a manifesto supporting the Conservatives on the grounds that 'the ILP openly associates with Trotskyists who were publicly convicted of acting as Hitler's agents in every country in the world'.[35] The following year they campaigned for the Tories against the ILP in a by-election in Cardiff East under the slogan 'A vote for Brockway is a Vote for Hitler' ('Stalinists Attack Left', in the *Militant*, new series no. 7, May, 1942). A duplicated leaflet given out for a meeting addressed by Idris Cox entitled *Brockway or Grigg?* called for a vote for the War Minister, since 'this is no ordinary by-election, the old party slogans count for nothing in the present situation'. They said a vote for the ILP would 'endanger the lives of our brave lads in the forces', whilst ILP policy of freedom for India would render it 'an easy prey for the Japanese invaders'. 'Sir James Grigg might not be a socialist', it went on, 'but he *does* want to beat Hitler. Fenner Brockway pretends to be a socialist; but his policy means *victory for Hitler.*' The advice of the Communist Party to the electors was '*far better vote for Sir James Grigg, the honest capitalist, than a false socialist*' (emphasis in original). 'The Communist Party', wrote a disappointed ILP candidate, 'is let loose at every by-election in support of Tory die-hards against men who have given a lifetime of service to the socialist cause'. Taking the title of his pamphlet from the 1936 election slogan of the Spanish Socialist Youth—'Defend Socialism from the Communists'—he appealed to Labour, ILP and Common Wealth supporters to unite to 'shake off the deadening influence of the spurious national unity and be rid of the corruption of Communist influence'.[36] And Communists were not without their qualms of conscience. As Harry Pollitt expressed it,

'We want to deal with some of the difficulties that are said to stand in the way of our Party members when they take part in by-elections and recommend the people to vote for a Government candidate—who happens to be a Tory.

Clearly it is not an easy task to carry out . . .

What is said to be the biggest obstacle in winning Labour workers to support our policy where the Government candidate is a Tory . . .'[37]

Communist assistance to the government was not limited to by-elections. Their members in trade unions tried to get them to issue libel writs against Socialist anti-war newspapers,[38] and to invoke the law against their publishers: 'the great labour movement would do well thoroughly to isolate them and work to operate 18b to put them where they rightfully belong—inside, next to Mosely and Hess.'[39]

A more disturbing case of collusion with the police came from Northern Ireland. Just before he was detained under the Special Powers Act for giving out leaflets, Bob Armstrong wrote to his friends in London: 'Some time ago, I received a report that the chief of the political police had asserted that I was linked up with the German delegation in Dublin. Yesterday in an interview he point-blank reiterated that view. He denied that the Stalinists had directly given "information" on this, but tacitly persuaded me to understand that they have their own method of allowing such "information" to filter through.'[40] His suspicions were confirmed when his comrade, Pat McKevitt, a citizen of Eire, was arrested on December 29th, 1942. Before anybody, even himself, knew what was about to happen to him, Betty Sinclair (a CP leader still active in those parts) was heard to comment that 'I understand from the authorities that they are going to send McKevitt back over the border'. It was a remarkable statement to make, as he was not allowed to see anyone when he was deported, not even his wife, and neither she, the solicitor, or the campaign committee knew that it had happened until he had gone.[41]

Meanwhile, the Communist Party redoubled its efforts to secure the legalisation of the *Daily Worker*. In the spring of 1942 the Daily Worker League held a conference to call for the removal of the Home Office ban. From the platform came heady speeches about democracy and the freedom of opinion. But an ILP shop steward and convenor delegated to the conference were not allowed to speak, still less move their amendment to the main resolution. Leaving the conference in disgust, they encountered CP stewards outside the hall giving other dissident socialists a lesson in freedom of opinion by tearing their papers from their hands and scattering them over the pavement.[42]

Finally, after the Labour Party Conference of May 1942 had called for the lifting of the ban, Herbert Morrison decided to allow the paper to reappear. Whether it was due to labour movement pressure or not is uncertain, as the Communists had already given proof of their new attitude in industry, and without their organ, as the *New Statesman* pointed out, 'as things stand, the Communists, and all those in the factories who are campaigning for increased production, have to fight the disruptionists with one hand tied behind their backs'.[43] At any rate, the paper hastened to give proof of loyalty in the very first of the new series, defining its aims as to 'speak for Britain, for a virile national unity, firmly buttressed by a united working class'.[44] As for Morrison, his thinly-disguised contempt remained. Other government circles shared his attitude when they refused to allow the paper's correspondent to accompany all the others at the Normandy landings that the CP were so enthusiastic about.[45]

On their side, the Communists maintained their intolerance towards others, for their enthusiasm for democracy of the capitalist variety did not extend to supporting democracy in the labour movement. They assaulted Trotskyist newspaper sellers outside a meeting addressed by Pollitt in Birmingham to such effect that the *Town Cryer*, the local Labour newspaper, splashed the story, protested to the Communists, and sent an observer to the next meetings to see that it was not repeated.[46] A woman in the ILP had her copies of the *New Leader* snatched from her hands and taken into a Communist Party meeting at the Stoll Theatre. The Chief Steward, Jack Gaster, denied all responsibility,[47] and an appeal to the

National Council for Civil Liberties (notoriously reluctant to take up
civil liberties cases after June 1941) only produced the advice that she
should write to the Communist Party.[48] They denied that Gaster or
any of his stewards had even been approached, and claimed that 'it is
impossible for us to trace any single individual who was outside a
meeting at which over 2,400 people attended'.[49] But the decision to
prevent oppositional views being aired outside their meetings had
been taken as a deliberate act of national policy; a party circular put
out on the 10th November, 1941, urged that

> 'The Trotskyist poison must be exposed and cleared out of the
> movement. The attitude of our Party membership has been too
> much one of culpable indifference and neglect. Even outside our
> own meetings Trotskyist literature has been freely sold without
> protest from our side; and the title of their scurrilous rag, calling
> itself *Socialist Appeal*, with the shouted slogan "Defend the Soviet
> Union", deceives innocent purchasers, because we do nothing to
> expose them and protect the workers against them.'[50]

This particular directive was aimed at the Workers' International
League, but when we remember how the CP regarded the ILP, and
even Labour Party members, as being under the influence of
'Trotskyism', we can well understand just what inroads upon free
expression inside the labour movement this policy entailed.

But practices of this type have been traditionally rejected inside the
trade unions and the Labour Party. Though most Labour supporters
were just as sincere in their enthusiasm for the war as were the
Communists, their good-humoured toleration of even the most
outlandish views protected many a dissident and gained a hearing for
him that he would not otherwise enjoy. They believed they were
fighting for democracy; and as far as they could see, that went at
home as well as abroad. Suppression of oppositional views by force
was fundamentally alien to their thinking, and left a nasty taste.
Communist behaviour in industry left another.

Footnotes

1 Churchill, speech in the Commons, 22nd June, 1941.
2 'Soviet-German Pact a Year Old', dateline Moscow, Friday 21st, in the *Daily
   Worker*, 24th August, 1940.

Daily Worker

ALLIES HAD "EVERYTHING PREPARED" FOR INVASION

HERE are the main points of yester-day's news, as reported by the Exchange Telegraph Company and from other sources:—

The Military Correspondent of the Exchange Telegraph in Paris says:— "The German invasion of the Low Countries is in no way took the Allied Command by surprise. The Allied Command has everything prepared. Eight months of preparation have brought the Allies' forces to a marvellous state of readiness."

The Belgian Premier declared in a speech yesterday:—"France and Great Britain have not broken their promises and are giving us, according to their guarantee, all military, naval and aerial support in their power. Holland, Luxemburg, and Belgium are united as never before in their history. Belgium has neglected nothing for her defence."

The appeal to the British and French Governments was made by King Leopold, Brussels wireless station announced yesterday.

IMMEDIATE STEPS

The British and French Governments officially announced that "they are taking immediate steps to come to the assistance of Belgium and Holland with all the means at their command.

"At the same time it must be recognised that once again Germany has gained a military advantage by taking the initiative in attacking neutral countries.

"The Germans have attempted to justify this act of aggression by alleging that Holland and Belgium have not preserved neutrality. This allegation is, of course, completely false.

"The Allies, who have taken all possible measures to provide for this eventuality in case of need, are now putting them into effect with the greatest speed."

"HOPED UNTIL LAST MINUTE"

M. Spaak, Belgian Foreign Minister, said: "We hoped until the last minute. Last night, at nine o'clock, we learned that German troops opposite the Belgian frontier had started marching. Then we understood. At four o'clock we learned that two Dutch airdromes had been bombed.

"A few minutes later we saw the first German bomber circling over Brussels from the window of the Foreign Office."

It is officially announced that arrangements have been made to assist the evacuation of British subjects from Holland and Belgium.

It is stated in Paris that the greater part of the huge gold stock of the Dutch and Belgian Governments had already been dispersed to the United States and elsewhere before the German invasion, and the gold which remained has now reached safety in France.

BRITISH CABINET MEETS

The British Cabinet met at 8 o'clock yesterday morning and sat for half an hour, and met again at 11.30. The Chiefs of Staff were present. There were large crowds in Downing Street. General Sir Edmund Ironside and Admiral Sir Dudley Pound were at No. 10 for an hour. Sir Cyril Newall, Chief of Air Staff, left a few minutes later.

The French Premier received the Ministers for Air and for the Colonies yesterday morning, then conferred for half an hour with the President of the Republic, then had a consultation with M. Louis Marin, the Right Wing Conservative leader, and afterwards with M. Herriot.

Later in the day, M. Reynaud, Premier, saw a number of other political leaders, and M. Daladier, the Minister for War, saw M. Bonnet, former Minister of Justice.

It was stated on the best authority that "these and other interviews are associated with the preliminary step being taken towards the reshuffling of the Cabinet."

Sensational rumours were in circulation regarding the character of the French Government "crisis," and the possibility of a move by the Laval-Flandin group.

Monday, September 11, 1939

DAILY WORKER

Editorial and Business Offices:
NELSON PLACE, CAYTON STREET,
LONDON, E.C.1.
Tele.: CLerkenwell 4781 (5 lines).
Business Grams: Workadaily,
Fleesquare, London.
Press Grams: DAILY WORKER, London.
DAILY WORKER League: 17, Duncan Terrace, London, N.1.
Telephone: TERminus 5714.

Scottish Office:
118, Broomielaw, Glasgow, C.1.
Telephone:
Glasgow CENtral 2653.
SUBSCRIPTION RATES:
7d. per week (late delivery).
10d. per week (early delivery).

MONDAY, SEPTEMBER 11, 1939

TO BETRAY POLAND IS TO BETRAY BRITAIN

THE expected Nazi peace offer has arrived via the speech of General Goering.

In effect, General Goering tells France and Britain, " You have been unable to protect Poland and you will be unable to break through our Western Front. Let's fix up a peace on the basis that we will be allowed to do what we like with Poland. In return we will guarantee your frontiers in the West."

That the situation is tragic for Poland will be denied by no one.

The question uppermost in every mind must be, " Was the Polish Government well advised to reject Soviet military assistance and so prevent the conclusion of a real pact of mutual assistance? About all was the British Government not neglectful of the interests of the British people and of peace in encouraging this attitude, instead of taking a most energetic stand against it?

Most people will agree with Mr. Lloyd George, who wrote quite bluntly yesterday with regard to the rejected Soviet plan for military aid to Poland. The tragic story of the rejection of this plan has yet to be told and the responsibility for the stupidities that lost us Russia's powerful support sternly dealt with." (Sunday Express, September 10.)

Goering's peace move is a very simple one. It is to suggest to the pro-Fascists in France and Britain that they can basely desert Poland without any harm coming to themselves. It is to suggest to the French that they are foolishly allowing themselves to be egged on by Britain into fighting a useless and unnecessary war.

Do not let us under-rate the strength of the forces which will be prepared to listen to this appeal.

A large number of " our betters " bolted like rabbits out of London immediately war was declared. And such people are influential. They will spread the propaganda everywhere that nothing remains but for France and Britain to bolt out of the war.

Don't let us overlook that much of the success obtained by the Nazis up to now has been based on a correct understanding of pro-Fascist big business in France and Britain.

And don't forget that Britain and France, instead of automatically coming in on Poland's side, when the German attack was unloosed, kept out of the war for two and a half precious days and would perhaps have kept out longer, if the misgiving of the British people had not found expression in Parliament on September 2.

FIGHT, WORK and SACRIFICE

The Daily Worker publishes today an important statement on the present situation which the Political Bureau of the Communist Party has issued to its members.

A NEW situation in the war has opened out, characterised by the launching of the Anglo-American offensive in Northern Africa; the successful Soviet holding of Stalingrad; the rising confidence and enthusiasm of the United Nations as they see the defensive phase beginning to give place to the offensive, and the confident note of Soviet utterances (but also implicit warning and emphasis of urgency) with regard to the favourable possibilities of a concerted Allied offensive.

Far-reaching possibilities open out from this offensive. The whole question of the Second Front in Europe—which continues more urgent and not less urgent—needs to be approached in a new and positive fashion in relation to this offensive.

We welcome the successes that have already been won, and we will do everything in our power to make it possible for complete success to be achieved for the full strategical objectives that are being sought.

the failure to establish the Second Front in Europe in 1943 did not attempt to controvert this clear statement of the facts.

The pledge with regard to a Second Front in Europe in 1943 was universally regarded by the British, American and Soviet peoples and by the nations of the world, as a pledge to be honoured. The subsequent explanation that it was a ruse to mislead the enemy cannot wipe out this colossal failure to adopt the necessary steps for victory in 1942.

THE holding back before the practical difficulties in establishing the Second Front in Europe during the summer and autumn of 1942 meant, in fact, a gamble on the capacity of the Soviet Union to hold out in isolation during all these months—and it is only the miracle of the Soviet achievement which has made possible the present situation.

The correctness of the Communist Party's campaign is thus all the more strongly proved by Mr. Churchill's statement. But our attention now needs to be concentrated, not on the controversies of the past, but on the present situation and the most rapid and effective utilisa-

Gen. B. L. MONTGOMERY, victor in Libya.

few leading military and naval personalities, such as Giraud, or Darlan, it is necessary to bring into the forefront the role which must be played by the French movement gathered around De Gaulle and the French National Council and the mass movement in France as our strongest allies

Middle East, would be prepared to leave Hitler in control of Europe. It is probable that, in the event of Allied success in Northern Africa, and of Hitler's failure to make headway in the East, Hitler may endeavour to appeal to those elements with offers of a compromise peace on the basis of maintenance of his conquests in Europe.

Whatever criticisms we have to make against the Churchill Government, there is one thing on which we need to be clear. That is that as a Government it does stand for the complete defeat of Hitler.

But at the same time the present situation makes it all the more necessary to strengthen the Government, and to press our demand for the replacement of all pro-Fascist and incompetent elements by the most effective democratic anti-Fascist representatives.

THEREFORE what should be the essence of our policy in the immediate situation? To set the example in the way we fight, work and sacrifice to make the African offensive a triumphant success. To obtain not only the maximum production, but to surpass any target

---

REMEMBER NELSON'S FAMOUS WORDS
'LET US GET TO WORK'

TRAFALGAR SQUARE is in the very heart of London. High above the granite figure stands the famous figure of Lord Nelson. On one day in late October, every year, his Majesty's Office of Works place wreaths about the base of Nelson's column. The honour the memory of Britain's greatest naval victory, the Battle of Trafalgar.

In 1805, Napoleon, tyrant of Europe and would-be master of the world, assembled a great army with transports at Boulogne, ready to invade Britain. He is alleged to have said: "Give me control of the Channel for six hours and I will settle the business." He was baulked—not by the Channel but by Lord Nelson and the British Fleet.

Nelson took the offensive, sought out Napoleon's fleet, and shattered it at Trafalgar. This victory paved the way for Napoleon's defeat by the Allies on land in Russia and at Waterloo.

TED BRAMLEY TELLS THE STORY OF LONDON AND STALINGRAD AND CALLS FOR THE MIGHTIEST SECOND FRONT DEMONSTRATION THAT TRAFALGAR SQUARE HAS EVER KNOWN.

Today Hitler, tyrant of Europe and would-be master of the world, concentrates his colossal army against the city of Stalingrad. Every day his spokesmen say: "Once Russia is crippled then we turn against Britain." Upon the outcome of that great battle and the fate future of mankind and a thousand cities, of London and a thousand cities.

"The supreme question is, however, will Britain transform the present danger into a great opportunity, as she did in 1805—by sailing out to attack the common enemy?

For eight weeks Londoners have anxiously scanned their papers. At the back of their minds is the nightmare memory of eight months of continuous night bombing. The memory of 20,000 Londoners blown to pieces, crushed to death, drowned in cellars. The memory of 24,000 Londoners maimed and mutilated. Such horrors as that of Balham tube station when people choked out their lives, drowned in the filth from a sewer cut by a bomb—will never be forgotten.

Remembering these things, the hearts of Londoners beat as

The greatness of a city is to be found not merely in its size, its cathedrals, its buildings, its wealth, its past history, or in its great contrasts. The source of a city's greatness is to be found in its people. Londoners are great people. The great majority working men and women. Neither tyranny at home nor abroad has cowed them. Neither unemployment, slums, poverty nor insecurity have stamped out their joy of life or love of liberty.

Always in these causes they have had to fight enemies in their own city. Always there have been working men and women ready to maintain these great traditions.

The London dockers stopped the "Jolly George" and helped to maintain the life of the young Soviet Republic. the Silvertown stevedores stopped the Haruna Maru when cold and unmoved about mained cold and unmoved China. Hundreds of London lads went to Spain, and many to die in Spain—when a craven Prime Minister feared "to burn his fingers."

But the eyes of the Stalingrad people are on London. Fifty times a day they ask: "When are our Allies going to open the Second Front?" Four months ago our Government, in our name, gave a solemn pledge. Now Joseph Stalin has bluntly called upon the Allies to "fulfil their obligations fully and on time." What is to be the answer? If we answer "Next year—some time," our names will be held in contempt by decent people throughout

---

tebook

he in his constituency a few days ago, proved himself unreprentant. A speaker at this meeting was Mr. P. I. Street, prospective Labour candidate, who vigorously denounced Mr. Donner as a pro-Fascist.

Somewhat to the public astonishment, Donner, in his fin speech

---

". . . their rightful place in the great tradition, the heritage which is theirs . . ."

3 *Challenge*, 14th June, 1941. Cf. R. Black, *Stalinism in Britain*, London, 1970, p. 144.
4 D. N. Pritt, 'The Churchill Coalition—and the Alternative', in *Labour Monthly*, June 1941, p. 261.
5 *Labour Monthly*, vol. xxiii, no. 7, July, 1941, pp. 33-6, 295.
6 H. Pollitt, *Letter to the Party Membership*, 8th July, 1941: 'For the Defeat of Fascism—An Appeal to our Party'
7 *Labour Monthly*, August, 1941.
8 *Daily Worker*, 27th May, 1940.
9 H. Pollitt, *Britain's Chance Has Come*, CPGB pamphlet, July, 1941, p. 6
10 Editorial Statement, *Daily Worker*, 7th September, 1942.
11 'Sayings of Mr. Churchill'—April 14th 1937, in the *Daily Worker*, 21st October, 1940.
12 R. Black, *Stalinism in Britain*, London, 1970, pp. 152-3.
13 *Daily Worker*, 11th October, 1940.
14 H. Pollitt, *Smash Hitler Now*, CPGB pamphlet, 26th June, 1941, p. 3.
15 H. Pollitt, *Britain's Chance Has Come*, CPGB pamphlet, July, 1941, p. 5.
16 *The British Labour Movement, the War, and the Communist Party*, 1941. Report of the 41st Annual Conference of the Labour Party, Westminster, May 1942, p. 7.
17 *The Labour Party and the Communist Party*, Statement of the NEC of the Labour Party, February, 1943, in the Report of the 42nd Annual Conference of the Labour Party, 1943, p. 228.
18 41st Annual Conference of the Labour Party, Westminster, May 1942. Official Report, p. 158.
19 Bert Atkinson, Interview with Sam Bornstein and Al Richardson, 10th November, 1977.
20 H. Pollitt, *Smash Hitler Now*, CPGB pamphlet, 26th June, 1941, p. 9.
21 E.g. W. Rust, *Victory This Year; Service for Victory; 12th National Congress of the YCL*, etc.
22 'Frank Pitcairn Reports' (Claude Cockburn), in the *Daily Worker*, 23rd December, 1942.
23 W. H. Wainwright, 'Fascist in Disguise', in *World News and Views*, vol. xxiii, no. 48, 27th November, 1943, pp. 459-460.
24 *Ibid.*
25 *Daily Worker*, 7th June, 1944.
26 'Money and Peace', editorial in the *Daily Worker*, 23rd May, 1944.
27 Editorial in the *Daily Worker*, 12th April, 1944.
28 W. Rust, 'Speaking for the Germans', in the *Daily Worker*, 21st July, 1944.
29 'No Fraternisation', editorial in the *Daily Worker*, 27th March, 1945.
30 Especially by R. Black, *Stalinism in Britain*, London, 1970, pp. 148-178, 179-191.
31 'Statement of H. Pollitt on D. F. Springhall', in the *Daily Worker*, 31st July, 1943.
32 H. Pollitt, *Appeal to Our Party*.
33 Official Report of the 41st Annual Conference of the Labour Party, Westminster, May 1942, p. 150.
34 'Bilston—Government has Less than 400 Majority', in the *Daily Worker*, 22nd September, 1944. The actual figures were:
    Arthur Easton (ILP) 9,344
    Lt. Col. W. E. Gibbons (Cons) 9,693
35 'Edinburgh Election: Communist Warning', in *World News and Views*, vol. xxi, no. 52, 27th December 1941, p. 826; John McNair, 'Fight for Socialism at Edinburgh', in the *New Leader*, vol. xxxiii, no. 40, 13th December, 1941.
36 Tom Taylor, *Defend Socialism Against the Communists*, ILP pamphlet, October 1942, pp. 3, 11. Cf. Brenan, *The Spanish Labyrinth*, Cambridge U.P., 1943, p. 307, etc.

37 H. Pollitt, Speech to the National Conference of the CPGB, May 1942, in *The Communist Party on the Way to Win*, p. 34 ('By Elections').

38 'Libel Writ to Gag Socialist Appeal', in *Socialist Appeal*, vol. iv, no. 8, May, 1942.

39 H. Kanner, letter of 1st October, 1943, in the *South London Press*.

40 Letter of 24th November, 1942, in 'Ulster Police Action Against Socialists', in *Socialist Appeal*, vol. v, no.5, February, 1943.

41 *Ibid.*

42 W. Hunter, 'Our Readers Say' (Letters to the Editor), in the *New Leader*, vol. xxxiv, no. 6, 18th April, 1942, p. 4.

43 *New Statesman*, 18th July, 1942.

44 'How to Win the War', Policy Adopted by the Editorial Board, *Daily Worker*, 9th September, 1942.

45 'This is a People's Invasion', in the *Daily Worker*, 7th June, 1944. Cf. above, p. 79.

46 Percy Downey, Interview with Sam Bornstein, 26th November, 1977.

47 'CP Try to Stop "New Leader" Sale', in the *New Leader*, 3rd January, 1942, p. 6.

48 Letter to Florence Stamp from the NCCL, 31st December, 1941.

49 London District Committee of the CPGB, letter to Florence Stamp, 16th January, 1942.

50 *The Fight for National Unity of the British-Soviet Alliance. Against Trotskyist Disruption. Against Leftist Confusions.* CPGB, 10th November, 1941, p. 3.

Chapter Six

At the Double: The Communists in Industry, 1941–5

The war years from 1941 on were the halcyon time of the British Communist Party. Its highest membership figure, 56,000, was obtained at the end of 1942. For the time being there was no clash between the foreign policy interests of the Soviet Union and the requirements of patriotism. It was still possible to applaud Churchill and the 'Soviet Heroes' in the same breath, from platforms for 'friendship with the USSR' all over the country, grouping together Tory councillors, establishment dignitaries, and trades union and Labour figures of varying hues. It was the Popular Front all over again, without the need to campaign for another government.

The services Communists could place at the government's disposal at elections and in parliament were limited by the electoral truce and the party's small representation. But what remained of their Marxist training told them that politics are not an affair of parties and governments alone, but determine the wider life of society, particularly relations entered into at the point of production. It was within industry and inside the Trades Unions that the Communists were able to make their greatest contribution to the alliance of the USSR and the Western powers, in support for the National Government, and in the maintenance of that class peace that alone would enable maximum war production. Here the party's advantage was unrivalled, for it could bring the full weight of its industrial apparatus, official trade union positions, front organisations and fellow travellers in all their ramifications to bear on the working class, backed by a state that was more powerful than ever before.

They threw themselves into this work with their eyes open, because all they had to do was adopt the sort of policies that they had spent the last few years denouncing. As J. R. Campbell had expressed it,

'Class co-operation in Britain would imply co-operation with the National Government—the political expression of big business in Britain.

It would imply the dampening down of the strike movements. The Communist Party is the most resolute opponent of both these policies.'[1]

His opinion was shared by Dutt, who two months previously had described views that strikes in wartime assist the enemy as 'familiar from the gutter sheets of Tory jingoism: the bottom pit of shame is reached when they are used by those who dare to call themselves "Socialists" '.[2] Most telling of all was a book written by Wal Hannington in 1940 (and reprinted in 1941), which had analysed the workers' experiences during the First World War and drawn revealing comparisons with the present. He had catalogued all the tricks of the employers and their Labour agents, including the 'big sacrifices' demanded by government and employers 'in the same manner as today',[3] Labour's 'political truce with the class enemy',[4] the breaking of 'existing trade union practices and working conditions', 'proposals for dilution of labour in the engineering shops', 'female labour and unlimited overtime',[5] illegalisation of strikes and imposition of compulsory arbitration,[6] the 'vitriolic' press campaign 'branding those who struck work in defence of their conditions as agents of the enemy',[7] and the hamstringing of the unions by their leaders for the duration of the war.[8] 'We are still living under the same economic system which induced such conduct in the last war', he wrote, 'and while that system remains we cannot feel secure against such disgraceful practices'.[9] 'Give up the right to strike under capitalism', he warned, 'and you forfeit the fundamental basis of trades unionism'.[10] Since all these were promoted by the Communists during this time, we can only conclude that it was a conscious policy adopted with a full understanding of exactly what it entailed in the short term and for the future. We must assume that the party threw itself into the 'bottom pit of shame' knowing just how deep it went.

Pollitt was laying the groundwork of the new policy only a month after the German invasion of the USSR by instructing the party member in industry to become (in effect) a management spy who 'will deal with domestic factors in regard to trade union practices, or alleged absenteeism in a manner present methods can never do'.[11] His suggestion for lifting industrial output was to import Stakhanovism from the Soviet Union, advising the BBC to 'let skilled workmen come and tell us what they think could be done to increase production'.[12] Party members in industry set about trying to put it into practice by forming 'shock brigades'.[13] The motive was exactly the same as in the Soviet Union, to justify speed-up and heightened exploitation by allowing management to point to the achievements of part of the workforce to be able to accuse the rest of laziness, or inefficiency.

Another import from the USSR was to rule out strikes altogether. 'We oppose strikes at the present time', Pollitt wrote after the great Barrow dispute, 'because they are against the present and future interests of the working class; and because existing trade union machinery, if rightly used, and backed up by public opinion, can bring results satisfactory to the workers without dislocating the productive process'.[14] It was exactly the sort of stuff the workers got every day from the newspapers—to put their faith in the official channels; that strikes only harm the workers themselves; and that they could not get anywhere without the support of a 'public opinion' manipulated by hostile mass media. An extra note of insincerity was furnished by the remark that 'we know that a continuation of strikes can prolong the war and help those who want to make a deal with Hitlerism', forgetting which was the first party to call for such a 'deal' in the first place.

Blanket rejection of the strike weapon was the cue for a vicious attack upon trade union rights, organisation and the defence of working conditions, as well as against all feelings of class solidarity and the elementary instincts of class consciousness. Pollitt went to the rostrum to justify scabbing at his party's 1942 Conference:

'I salute our comrade, a docker from Hull, who was on a job unloading a ship with a cargo urgently wanted . . . When the rest of the dockers struck work, he fought against it because he believed that the course of action he recommended would get what was wanted without a strike. What courage, what a sacred spirit of real class consciousness, to walk on the ship's gangway and resume his job . . .'[15]

Unavoidably, the nationalism that accompanied this sort of thing gave rise to the most reactionary sentiments. 'If a man doesn't pull his weight in war production, then, whether he is a labourer or an engineer, he should be put in the army' was one remark passed at a Communist shop stewards' meeting and not, as it would seem at first sight, a royal birthday celebration of blimpish colonels.[16] The party was not anxious to see that the workman got an adequate return for his labour. 'The civilian population may have to go shorter than at present for fuel and food', noted William H. Wainwright, but privation would be followed by pious rewards, for 'once the Second

Front is in operation the whole country will be uplifted as if by a new spirit'.[17] In the meantime, the CP did its best to tie the workers to the official machinery, to delay, entangle, or confuse the issue— anything other than allow industrial strife. 'The success attending deputations of workers to local authorities, Ministries and Members of Parliament indicates that it is possible to win our demands without resort to strike action' ran a report to the CP conference of 1942.[18]

Whilst Pollitt laid the basis for strategy in industry, its elaboration into a system was the preoccupation of J. R. Campbell, who took time off to do it from his other obsession with the 'Hitlerism with a red tie' of the ILP or the Trotskyists. The first draft of his work appeared in a special issue of *Labour Monthly* in December 1941. What was needed, he affirmed, was a 'strong government' of Tories, Liberals and Labour, which required a 'great popular movement for solidarity with the Soviet Union' to ensure it fulfilled its obligations. 'If Hitler won', he added, it 'would not merely be a question of the British state losing this or that Imperial possession', but of the 'physical extermination' of 'the British People'. The ILP's demand for 'replacing the Churchill Government by a Socialist Government' was 'black treachery'. So repeating scare propaganda of the ruling class he justified dilution, increased production and a carefully elaborated plan for class collaboration. Going through it, he could not avoid the sort of complaints usual on the lips of managers, about idle workers, 'restrictive practices', 'ignorant and conservative' trade union attitudes, 'old customs and practices', and ' "so-called Socialists" ' who 'shout betrayal' when a speaker at a Shop Stewards' Conference suggests that workers engaged in producing tanks and planes should not idle their time away'.[19]

It was Campbell's alibi for an attack upon defences elaborated by generations of trade unionists against speed-up, wage-cutting, and grinding exploitation. Practices going back for centuries were dismissed in airy management language as 'a petty corporate custom' (often of no real value as far as being a bulwark of present-day working conditions is concerned)',[20] persisting through an 'ignorant and conservative spirit'. His use of the word 'conservative' whilst supporting the Tory Prime Minister of the day was quite odd to find, along with accents of a factory manager faced with his men's resistance to 'increased production' and 'new methods' in industry. 'Restrictive practices', he went on, 'are a relic of craft unionism', and 'whether we like it or not, we are in for vast changes in industry, which cannot be met by clinging to old customs and practices'.[21]

Campbell knew the men's point of view, even if it did not carry too much weight with him:

'One can understand why the craftsmen in certain districts (who sacrificed a great deal in the last war, only to find the employers and government forgetting what they had promised as soon as the war was over) being chary about the introduction of women and trainees into industry, and should look askance at suggestions for increasing production. Their attitude is the result of bitter experience.'[22]

But he drew entirely different lessons from history than they did. The war was 'an entirely new experience', he explained, waged 'against a power that aims to destroy all trade unions'. He was upset to discover that many working men of different views did not appreciate this. 'The old fashioned trade unionist who wants to leave production questions to the management and concentrate only on wages and conditions is backed up by being told that for workers to concern themselves with managerial questions before the Socialist revolution is "class co-operation" ',[23] he complained. It was a confession that the industrial policy of the Communists was to the right of the most conservative class-conscious trade unionists. They agreed that the war was for the defence of democracy, but they could see no point sacrificing that trade union organisation they regarded as its greatest benefit. Indeed, the alliance of the Communist Party with management was gradually producing a counter-alliance of the skilled men and the politicised militants. 'It is notorious', wrote Campbell, 'that in certain workshops the "Lefts" are seeking an alliance with the most conservative sections of the trade union movement on the basis of opposition to any attempt to increase production'.[24]

Campbell's article was one of a collection designed to make that number of Labour Monthly a handbook for the Communists' offensive against the trade union movement. Bound up along with it were a circular from the Employers' Federation approving of Production Committees, and a sophisticated and practical guide to class collaboration from the pen of Len Powell. He knew full well what he was doing when he wrote that 'Shop stewards, representing the point of view of their members, together with charge hands and foremen meeting regularly with the managements, can bring forward the best and quickest methods for doing jobs, which means that where managements are capable and responsive, much more production results'.[25] His article included many examples of the activities of the Communist-promoted Production Committees, of which we have space here for only a few:

'London Engineering Firm'

'Works are open for a minimum of 57½ hours per week, no weekend work. Men have agreed to discipline themselves to a minimum of 55 hours per week. Men have also agreed to cut the dinner-time clocking-in grace by 2 mins., also to cut time allowed for washing from 5 mins to 3 mins . . .'

'S. E. England Aircraft'

'At a recent interview with the management on production it was agreed that Harry Pollitt should be invited to address a meeting on production in the canteen . . . A minimum of 3 nights per week overtime and Saturday afternoon has been agreed on by several departments. Disciplinary action to be taken against any worker if men in department ask for action . . . (statement signed by a departmental foreman) . . . Overtime is being worked by the men and jobs are being done nearly twice as quick. One job which originally took 109 hours to do is now done in 47 hours by the same labour.'

'N. W. England'

'. . . Craft problems stand in the way and call for careful handling. Men have been known to side-step teaching girls or giving them the proper training. But these difficulties are now being sifted down to individuals . . .'

'S. W. London Instrument Works'

'. . . We have an efficient and reasonable management, but several unsuitable foremen. The main obstacles unfortunately lie on our side, due to apathy and anarchistic attitude of a number of employees . . .'

'West of London Factory'

'. . . Management informs Production Committee that clerical staff cannot take on extra work to get extra production, that we shall be producing 30 per cent more by next March: that they sympathise with our desire but that it is a national question . . .'

Powell was beside himself when a strike threatened to halt production. When 7,000 foundry workers at the Powell Duffryn works in South Wales struck work he went down in his capacity as Secretary of the 'Engineering and Allied Trades Shop Stewards' National Council' to persuade them to go back. When he turned up at a local meeting of the shop stewards he so antagonised them that they turned him out with a flea in his ear.[26]

Communist policy at work was most dangerous in the engineering industry. They had important positions within the union, especially in the London area, where they owed their prestige to a successful drive for unionisation which they had led before the war. Their implantation was firmer here than in any other sector, one vital to the prosecution of the war through production of ships, aircraft, arms and munitions. They dominated the Engineering and Allied Trades Shop Stewards' National Council, which they converted into 'the most enthusiastic supporter of higher productivity, and the fiercest opponent of unofficial strikes'.[27] Important here was a shop steward at Napier's, Walter Swanson, who ran a series of articles in the Labour Monthly during the autumn of 1941 under the heading of 'How to Increase War Production'. He aimed to win the workers in every factory for the maximum possible effort, in his words to 'get the workers to work the maximum hours compatible with health and efficiency'.[28]

A key part of his scheme was the organisation of a production conference of the Shop Stewards' National Council at the Stoll Theatre in London on October 19th, 1941. Among the 'sensational changes in traditional methods' he recommended were 'greater readiness to promote the changeability of labour', 'different trades to agree on prevention of demarcation rules restricting output', 'skilled workers to lead in devising new methods of work as jobs are broken up into a series of lesser skilled operations', and to 'set the highest example in the quantity, quality and rapidity with which they turn out the job'.[29] The main resolution at the gathering instructed stewards 'to report to mass meetings of our members as quickly as possible the discussions and decisions of this conference, using them as a guide and incentive to immediately increase production'.[30] It was done with a cynicism almost unparalleled in the history of the working class, such as when the party's noted labour historian, Allen Hutt, described the Stoll affair as 'enough, surely, to make the founding fathers of the old A.S.E. turn in graves: but something that Frederick Engels would have understood and approved—did he not urge the craft unions over fifty years ago to scrap the "old lumber" of their even then outworn craft prejudices and exclusiveness?'[31]

Swanson certainly tried to do his share to break down these 'prejudices'. He began in his own factory at Napiers' by proposing a pass-out system such as existed in some other factories, whereby anyone doing overtime had to seek the foreman's permission if he wanted to leave in less than two hours. Then he tried to lengthen the night shift by altering the timing of the supper break to increase the actual amount of overtime worked. This time a huge shop floor meeting stopped him with a blank refusal.[32] When another factory in the same group in Liverpool struck over the transfer of 23 of the men to a job on £1 less a week, Swanson sent a telegram on behalf of the Acton works—'DON'T STRIKE. PLAYING HITLER'S GAME'. Of course the men took no notice, and shortly afterwards won all their demands.[33]

The Stoll affair was only a start. Campbell pressed for the 'rationalisation' of the shipbuilding industry through the closure of a dozen drawing offices and the prefabrication of materials to undercut craftsmen's wages. Builders, shipbuilders and even miners were treated to little homilies about the need for the dispersal of tasks and the interchangeability of labour, supporting state direction of miners from place to place, and craftsmen being made to do labourers' jobs.[34] Jack Owen wrote a book for the instruction of managers in the proper application of time and motion techniques:

'A typical experiment was made in the case of a labourer whose job it was to unload pig iron from rail trucks. Over an eight-hour day, he was supervised by a man with a stop-watch, who gave instructions on how long to work and when. At the end of the day, his normal output had been trebled.'[35]

All over the country Communists jumped into action to enforce speed-up. At the Invicta Radio Company they brought up the question of absenteeism and lateness when they proposed a special committee of two managers and two shop stewards to 'examine' cases of them.[36] In the Rover plant in Birmingham a CP convenor called Crump actually got the sack for pestering the management constantly about idle men, machines and materials. When the local AEU shop stewards held their biggest ever district meeting to protest about it and voted for a one day sit-down strike, Crump was obliged to get up and oppose it, and to ask a later meeting to forget the whole thing![37]

Poor Crump! While he was a laughing stock, another CP convenor of a Merseyside aircraft factory named Ward was entertaining Sir Stafford Cripps and receiving the British Empire Medal for work on Production Committees.[38] At Cammell Lairds the Communists succeeded in introducing piecework where it had never existed before.[39] In one aircraft works in North London the Communist-controlled Shop Stewards' Committee worked frantically to help the management smash a strike voted for by 15,000 workers.[40]

They played every card in the pack to divide, demoralise and pit sections of the working class against each other. One of the party's women organisers, Isabel Brown, had still been complaining in 1940 that

'Already in the first months of the war, heavy burdens have been laid on the working women. Homes and families are broken up. Women are driven into munitions factories.'[41]

And worse was to come: 'they say that *four million* women will be required to leave their homes and enter industry and other occupations'.[42] By the time 1942 came round she was writing:

'A million are already on war work . . . But why are there only one million women employed in this way? Time after time we have been informed that the country needs *at least four million* extra women workers.'[43]

The women were used for dilution. J. R. Campbell advocated a 'firm attitude' to those who objected to it, 'backward workers who refuse to help the women in their work'. He tried to turn the clock back to the eighteenth century in the pits, making it 'possible in the mining industry for women to be employed on the surface to a great extent, thus releasing men *and boys* for work underground'.[44] But encouragement of female labour did not go with a policy of equal pay. When a new national agreement raised the rate of pay for women inspectors, the management of the Rolls Royce factory in Glasgow provoked a strike by issuing cards regrading them to the lowest grade. But the Communist-dominated Shop Stewards Committee refused to elect a strike committee, recommended a return to work, and even refused information to a deputation sent up from the Midlands factories in the same group of companies![45] There was not much sympathy, either, for the double exploitation of working women at home and in the factory. An item appearing in the *Daily Worker* under the heading of 'Then She Went Home and Did the Washing' related how

'Mrs. Nellie Mears, Bull Road, Selly Oak, Birmingham, has beaten the world's record of 1,700 shell components in 11 hours put up by another Birmingham capstan operator, Mrs. Evelyn Duncan. Mrs. Mears' figure was 1,800 in 10 hours. Then she went home and did her family washing. Aged 33, Mrs. Mears has two children. Her husband also makes munitions.'[46]

A month later the paper was giving publicity to a demonstration of women 'with husbands or sons in the Mercantile Marine or in the Navy' who had marched on a strike meeting on Tyneside to demand a return to work.[47]

Communist activity in the mining industry carried physical dangers with it. Though speed-up is accompanied by grave safety risks Campbell suggested competitions between collieries and areas: 'surely it is possible for each pit and district to challenge the other as to which will most exceed the target figure in a given period of time'.[48] Communists had a callous attitude to the slaughter in the pits: as a resolution expressed it,

> 'Coal production in the industry can be increased by regular working of all shifts available, eliminating all avoidable absenteeism, continuation of work after fatal accidents, and the relaxation of overtime restrictions . . .'[49]

They were serious about these measures. Where they had mass following, such as in Scotland, they used their influence to implement them:

> 'The Lothian miners' decision to work a special Sunday shift in honour of the division (the 51st Highlanders at El Alamein) is a generous, spontaneous acknowledgement of the achievements of their brothers in the forces.
> It is an example for all workers elsewhere.'[50]

Even traditional gestures of sympathy and humanity had to go to the wall. 'It was the custom for the whole pit to stop when a fatal accident took place,' one article ran approvingly, 'The Douglas miners have now decided to forego this custom'.[51] Worst of all was Horner, Communist leader of the South Welsh Miners. 'There is too much avoidable absenteeism in the mines, particularly on Saturdays and Mondays', he wrote, 'it should be regarded as a crime to the 1st and 8th Armies and to the Red Army not to work every available shift, including weekend overtime in the present period of crisis. The avoidance at all costs of strikes and the suspension of the custom where a pit closes down after a fatal accident would greatly increase production.'[52] Communist activity in the mines was so well-known that Jack Tanner referred to it in the debate on their party's affiliation to the Labour Party at the end of the war:

> 'Quite frankly, I think that the Government, and particularly the Minister of Fuel and Power, would have been very much more

embarrassed in regard to coal production if it had not been for the efforts of the Communists in the coalfield. I believe that it is safe to say that the position would have been very much worse if it had not been for the efforts of men like Arthur Horner.'[53]

The full weight of the law was threatened against those who advocated, or practised, striking in the coalfields. D. N. Pritt, QC, defined it as sowing 'dissension between the armed forces' and 'ordinary citizens', and 'the gravest possible injury to civil liberty, and to every other national interest'.[54] When one magistrate was humane enough to let a boy off with a caution for failing to go down the pit, the Daily Worker came out in protest:

'The law was being brought into contempt by a magistrate who declined to admonish a boy who refused his call to the coalmines. This has been followed by two other courts. What are we to think of magistrates whose action is equivalent to encouraging youngsters to refuse to share the legal duty that Parliament has asssigned to them and that the country needs?'[55]

It was a record of inhumanity against those condemned to work in a dangerous, exhausting and inefficient industry, whose employers themselves were not noted for their fellow feeling. But the Communists even argued that their services entitled them to special consideration from the Minister of Labour. 'Permit me to tell you, Mr. Bevin' wrote the Daily Worker editor after the great Barrow Strike, 'that but for the untiring efforts of Communist leaders in the mining industry—the men whom you describe as 'fleas'—there would have been long ago a state of chaos in the coalfields of Britain.'[56]

Their new policy placed them alongside the management and in opposition to militant trade unionists of every description. They utilised their industrial machinery to the full to denounce and victimise their opponents wherever possible, boasting of their activities in the national newspapers. One such, under the heading of Workers' Own Secret Society Hunts Traitors, quoted an anonymous 'shop steward official' describing 'the tiny band of politically inspired people' who were a 'cancer in the splendid body of the British war effort'. 'So the loyal workers', he went on, 'are taking the law into their own hands. They have organised their own secret service. They report in detail the activities and history of every suspected worker. They sit in secret judgement and fairly try him. And then they present their case to the managements.' So where the party was especially strong, in engineering and in the home counties, they had an immediate impact. 'In the South, particularly in the London area, they have cleaned out the saboteurs. Managements have helped by dismissing or having transferred workers who have been proved to be a hindrance.'[57] No imagination was needed to see the centre of the 'Workers' Own Secret Society' at the Party HQ in King Street. William H. Wainwright admitted as much when defending the Communist-backed 'Pit Production Committees' against ILP charges that they were 'an unpaid police force', when he remarked that 'perhaps that is because in some instances vigilant workers have reported the activities of pro-Nazi Trotskyists in the coal fields'.[58] On Tyneside they circulated a questionnaire around their 'contacts' asking for details of the politics of the chairmen and secretaries of trade union branches, so provoking the Executive of Wallsend AEU that they proposed debarring Communists from holding any further office on the Union's District Committee.[59]

The experience of one of the authors at Napier's factory in West London can serve as an illustration of the techniques used, and of what the men felt about it:

'I was already a member of the AEU, having joined in Coventry, and was then in the King's Cross branch with Dave Granick. The CP line was becoming more and more chauvinist, and at this stage they still carried with them the old trade union craftsmen, who were pro-war, in any case. I sold a few copies of Socialist Appeal in the factory, and was quickly approached by Ken Potter, a young worker who had served his time at Napier's as an apprentice. Politically, he was influenced by the ILP, and he and his wife had been active in the Co-op Guilds. I had no standing in the factory; I had not served an apprenticeship, and to the skilled workmen the attraction was non-existent.

Ken quickly joined the WIL group and had his own circle of people to whom he sold the Socialist Appeal. They were mainly young skilled workers, like Ken but non-political or hostile to the CP because they were encouraging the destruction of their old standards with dilutees and women membership. The older craftsmen still had a respect for them because they had organised the Napier Combine some years earlier.

The younger craftsmen knew little about this, and cared less. They only saw the CP as it was then. When I was elected a shop steward the Stalinists felt they had to do something, and they threatened to report me under Defence Regulations, which made it a criminal offence to sell or circulate anti-war literature in a factory. When I told Ken what was happening, the Stalinist Convenor, who was a member of the London District

Committee of the CP, was cornered by a group of workers, who threatened to beat him up if I was arrested. The poor fellow protested his innocence, saying *he* had no intention of reporting me. He was told that it didn't matter to them *who* did this reporting, he personally would be beaten up one dark night—and all the nights were dark!

Not long after this I was approached by another worker, who told me he had joined the CP, and had been buying the *Socialist Appeal* from me for some time. He had been told by the Stalinist fraction in the factory to get friendly with me and get some "dirt" on me. He was ashamed of this, and said he "wanted to confess". I asked him if he was a Catholic, and of course he was—and so the guilty conscience and confession. I then asked what "dirt" he did get, and he said "None. The *Socialist Appeal* puts a very straightforward case", but he had thought that there might be some more clandestine activity behind it.

Amongst our supporters there was an old German CPer. He and all of his brothers had been leaders of the CP—one had been a delegate to the Sixth World Congress in 1928, and leader of the Berlin Tramway Strike of 1932. He became disillusioned with Stalinism whilst a refugee in Czechoslovakia, when he noticed that any dissidents among the refugees would be given the honour of carrying out illegal work in Germany, and then disappearing. By the time he reached England, just before the war, he was openly critical of Stalinism.

The CP spread the story that he was a Nazi, and as he was non-Jewish, and had been interned in the early days, we were afraid he might be interned again. Through Ken we contacted Brockway, and as there were a number of anti-CP Socialists, Brockway took up his case with the Home Office. So nothing happened to him, or his wife, who had been an Austrian, a member of the Schützbund.'[60]

The impact of the CP's ideas on the working class was demoralising. Those who were used to hearing the Communists denounced as revolutionaries and troublemakers, now heard them speak in the voices of management and government. Campbell, again, was most crude in his echo of the official propaganda. 'It would be criminal', he wrote, 'if, when confronted with some workshop grievance, we were to adopt methods for securing a remedy such as strikes, that ignore the paramount needs of the war.'[61] For how many times have we not read in the yellow press, (then and since), that 'it is not true that increased production will rebound only to the interests of the capitalist' An increased production of coal will benefit us all this winter . . .' or that 'a working class engaged on a great production drive can get most of its grievances by publicity and by negotiation without in any way imperilling the flow of production'.[62] Similarly, any suggestions for nationalisation, workers' control, equality of sacrifice or the elimination of private profit were dismissed as 'specious anti-production claptrap', put out by the 'opponents of production'. These were variously described as 'certain labour men', 'old-fashioned trade unionists', and 'new-fangled revolutionary phrasemongers', who 'instead of insisting that Labour stays in the government and fights, want to ignominiously withdraw, thereby splitting the government and giving the worst reactionaries in the country their opportunity'.[63]

It was no boast when Pollitt claimed that 'it is the class conscious workers (sic!) in Britain inspired by the Communist Party, who have led the fight for increased production and to make the Joint Production Committees work, have been ready to accept dilution, forego hard-earned customs and practices in industry'.[64] But many trade unionists had other ideas.

Footnotes

1 J. R. Campbell, *Questions and Answers*, CPGB pamphlet, 28th March 1938, p. 20.
2 R. Palme Dutt, 'Notes of the Month', in *Labour Monthly*, vol. xxiii, no. 4, April 1941, p. 154.
3 Wal Hannington, *Industrial History in Wartime*, London, 1940, p. 24.
4 *Op. cit.*, p. 25.
5 *Op. cit.*, pp. 26-7; *cf.* p. 38.
6 *Op. cit.*, p. 48.
7 *Op. cit.*, pp. 34, 65, 94.
8 *Op. cit.*, p. 37.
9 *Op. cit.*, pp. 93-4.
10 *Op. cit.*, p. 97.
11 H. Pollitt, *Britain's Chance Has Come*, CPGB pamphlet, July, 1941, p. 12.
12 H. Pollitt, 'The Way to Victory', in *Labour Monthly*, vol. xxiii, no. 10, October 1941, p. 419.
13 *He Fights for Coal as He Fought in Spain*, in the *Daily Worker*, 15th September, 1942.
14 H. Pollitt, 'Industrial Unrest and its Causes', in *World News and Views*, 9th October, 1943.
15 H. Pollitt, Reply to Discussion, CPGB Conference, May, 1942.
16 *World News and Views*, xxi, 676.
17 W. H. Wainwright, *The Final Offensive*, CPGB pamphlet, 20th January, 1944, p. 6.

18 'Strikes', in the *The Communist Party on the Way to Win*, Decisions of the National Conference of the CPGB, 23rd May, 1942, p. 19.
19 J. R. Campbell, 'How "Leftism" Helps Hitler', in *Labour Monthly*, vol. xxiii, no. 12, December 1941, p. 494.
20 *Op. cit.*, p. 495.
21 *Ibid.*
22 *Ibid.*
23 *Ibid.*
24 *Op. cit.*, p. 494.
25 Len Powell (Secretary of the Engineering and Allied Trades Shop Stewards' National Council), 'Joint Production Committees', in *Labour Monthly*, vol. xxiii, no. 12, December, 1941, p. 486.
26 'Mass Action Among Welsh Engineers', in *Shop Stewards Pamphlet No. 1*, published by Don McGregor on behalf of the industrial committee of the ILP, p. 4.
27 H. Pelling, *A History of British Trades Unionism*, London, 1963, p. 215.
28 W. Swanson, 'How to Increase War Production', in *Labour Monthly,* vol. xxiii, no. 10, October, 1941, p. 439, points 1 and 3.
29 A. Hutt, 'Production—Key to Victory', in *Labour Monthly*, vol. xxiii, no. 11, November, 1941, p. 457, etc.
30 'For Increased Production', in 'Documents of the Month', *Labour Monthly*, vol. xxiii, no. 11, November, 1941. p. 447.
31 *Cf.* note 29 above.
32 Ajit Roy, 'Joint Production Committee—Bosses' Tools: Swanson Puts Bosses Case', in *Socialist Appeal*, vol. iv, no. 6, March 1942 pp. 1-2.
33 'Napiers Win Strike Victory', in *The Militant*, new series no. 4, January, 1942.
34 J. R. Campbell, *Your Part in History: An Appeal to Workers in the Mining, Shipbuilding, Engineering and Building Industries*, pamphlet issued by the Scottish District Committee of the CPGB (undated).
35 Jack Owen, *War in the Workshop*, June 1942, p. 48.
36 'Invicta Radio Limited', in *Workshop News*, published by the Industrial Committee of the Workers' International League, no. 1, June, 1942.
37 'Communist Party Helps Bosses to Victimise Its Own Members', in *Workshop News* no. 2, July, 1942, pp. 5-6.
38 *Socialist Appeal*, vol. v, no. 17, Mid-August, 1943.
39 *Socialist Appeal*, vol. iv, no. 7, April, 1942.
40 *Socialist Appeal*, vol. v, no. 17, Mid-August, 1943.
41 Isabel Brown, *Women and the War*, CPGB pamphlet, 1940, p. 3 (our emphasis).
42 *Op. cit.*, p. 12 (our emphasis).
43 Isabel Brown, *Women! Man the Factory Front*, CPGB pamphlet, 1942, p. 3 (our emphasis).
44 J. R. Campbell, *Your Part in History: An Appeal to Workers in the Mining, Shipbuilding, Engineering and Building Industries*, pamphlet of the Scottish District Committee of the CPGB (undated).
45 Tom Burns (Jock Haston), '25,000 Strike Defeat: Women's Wages to Undercut Men. CP aids bosses in blow at AEU', in *Socialist Appeal*, vol. v, no. 23, Mid-November, 1943, *cf.* 'Why Rolls Struck', in the *New Propellor*, organ of the CP in the Engineering Industry, December, 1943; Harry McShane, '2,000 Women Workers Strike', in the *Daily Worker*, 31st December, 1943.
46 'Then She Went Home and Did the Washing', in the *Daily Worker*, 10th September, 1942.
47 'Go Back! Say Women', in the *Daily Worker*, 8th October, 1942.
48 J. R. Campbell, *Your Part in History: An Appeal to Workers in the Mining,*

Shipbuilding, Engineering and Building Industries, pamphlet published by the Scottish District Committee of the CPGB, no date.

49 CPGB Resolution on Production, 18th September, 1942.

50 'Miners' Tribute', in the *Daily Worker*, 1st December, 1942.

51 'Miners Respond to Invasion Needs. Coal Output Rising', in the *Daily Worker*, 20th June, 1944.

52 *Daily Worker*, 19th December, 1942.

53 Jack Tanner (AEU), Speech to the 45th Conference of the Labour Party, Bournemouth, 10th-14th June, 1946—official report, p. 173.

54 D. N. Pritt, *Defence Regulation 1aa*, National Council for Civil Liberties pamphlet, 1941, p. 4.

55 'Strange Law', Second Editorial of the *Daily Worker*, 19th May, 1944.

56 W. Rust, 'An Open Letter to the Minister of Labour from the Editor', in the *Daily Worker*, 5th October, 1943.

57 'Our Industrial Correspondent', 'Workers' Own Secret Society Hunts Down Traitors', press cutting, Bornstein Archive.

58 'W. W.', 'Pro-Nazi', in *World News and Views*, no. 29, 16th July, 1942.

59 *New Leader*, vol. xxxiv, no. 43, 2nd January, 1943, p. 5.

60 Sam Bornstein, account written for this book, 25th October, 1977.

61 J. R. Campbell, *Your Part in History: An Appeal to Workers in the Mining, Shipbuilding, Engineering and Building Industries*, pamphlet published by the Scottish District Committee of the CPGB, undated.

62 *Op. cit.*, p. 9.

63 *Op. cit.*, p. 4.

64 H. Pollitt, *How to Win the War*, CPGB pamphlet, September, 1944, p. 15.

Chapter Seven

Disaffection in the Ranks: Communists and the Labour Revolt, 1942-45

Industrial militancy, submerged at the beginning of the war in a flood of patriotic feeling, began to pick up slowly in the course of 1942 and from then on to the close of hostilities began to mount into a major crisis. Communists themselves had done their best to encourage it until June, 1941, and it was unfortunate that the the moment they changed their policy to support for the war, the working class were losing their own enthusiasm for it. The labour revolt was due to particular structural problems in industry and war-weariness, as well as the general crisis that had been maturing since 1931. From the defeat of that year the movement had been gradually rising to its feet, in terms of both trade union militancy and electoral support for Labour. It was a slow recovery, with many ups and downs, but it was nonetheless sure. The coming of war in 1939, with all that it implied in terms of electoral truce and industrial peace, had halted, cut across and delayed this process, for a while. The expansion of the war and the intensification of the war effort after 1941 had finally brought it to a head. This was especially the case in those two sectors that were crucial for the production of war materials, engineering and mining.

The special needs of the war had led to a rapid expansion of the engineering industry, as the demand for munitions, armaments and ships began to mop up the pool of a million unemployed that had persisted throughout the thirties. For a while the AEU became the second largest union in the country, when its numbers more than doubled, from 334,000 in 1939 to 825,000 in 1943. The most significant change inside it had been the decision to admit women made in 1942, which had resulted in the recruitment of 139,000 in the first year. Fresh layers of militants had come forward who had spent much of the thirties without a job, and had lost little of the resentment they had gained from that experience. By 1941 they had been able to become elected to positions of responsibility in the union at a local level, such as shop stewards. The problem of the employers, on their part, was to attract enough labour into a rapidly expanding industry without cutting too deeply into the vast profits they were making out of government contracts by raising wages too much. It was not until late in 1943 that lay-offs returned, when competition from the immense arms production of the United States began to make inroads into the domestic market.

The union leadership had conceded the position before so much as a shot had been fired when they had signed the joint agreement of August 29th, 1939 with the Allied Employers' Federation to relax exisiting trade customs. In 1939, and after 1941, they had been greatly assisted in this policy by the support of the Communists, who had built up a formidable following in the union before the war, and filled many important positions within it at a national and a local level. As Jack Tanner put it when seconding the resolution at Labour Party Conference on Communist affiliation:

> 'As I think most of you are aware, during the war the shop stewards in the engineering industry played a very important part in increasing production through the Joint Production Committees, and it is, I think, generally known that a very huge proportion of the leading shop stewards in the engineering industry are Communists. We urgently need a similar enthusiasm and a similar movement to that which we had during the war. . .'[1]

The first gusts of the storm broke out in the Royal Ordnance Factory in Nottingham, where the Ministry of Labour tried to transfer 400 skilled men to private enterprise at lower rates of pay. As the convenor, chairman and branch secretary (and some of the shop stewards) were Trotskyists they had no inhibitions about leading the men in militant action. Not only did they gain the support of the union's local district committee and several neighbouring shop stewards' and works committees, but the AEU Executive itself refused to countenance the transfer of their men to any other type of factory than Royal Ordnance works. On April 18th, 1942, the 2,500 workmen occupied the factory for a two-day stay-in strike.

The local Communist shop stewards were too closely connected with the men to oppose this action, but the national leadership were outraged at what was, after all, a munitions strike at the height of the war. Soon J. R. Campbell appeared in the area with a sort of roving brief as an industrial trouble-shooter, and local CP industrial groups received instructions to send delegates to a committee formed to struggle against 'Trotskyists in the West Midlands'. Very quickly there appeared a leaflet in the factory entitled

COMMUNIST PARTY STATEMENT ON TRANSFERENCE OF LABOUR

'Does the transference of labour in a People's War justify strike action?

Does the transference of the Armed Forces engaged in battle against the enemy justify desertion?

We must not allow such questions as being transferred to another factory to hold up the guns, planes and ammunition that will help to remove the Nazis from the face of the earth. This may mean sacrifices, but nothing compared to the sacrifices made by our comrades in the Armed Forces who have left home, jobs and comfort to fight Fascism. . .'

The leaflet all but destroyed what credit the Communist Party still possessed in the factory. As one of the shop stewards expressed it in a letter to another working in the ROF group, 'You say that in your factory they are in decline. Well here they are in the shit, not to mention the decline. . .'[2]

Though the strike was kept out of the national dailies, the Communists' reaction was predictable, if muted. 'There is a small group of people at work in our ordnance factories' whimpered the *Daily Worker*, 'who, unless dealt with without delay, will seriously affect the production of vital munitions of war'. They appealed to the authorities, to 'pay some attention to the activities of the small bunch of saboteurs who, although not influential at the moment, can cause much harm if their activities are not curtailed'.[3]

Five months later trouble broke out in the Tyne shipbuilding yards, when the unions involved agreed to a management proposal to alter 'total time' from Thursday to Saturday without consulting the workforce. A bitter strike broke out over the loss, described by the *Daily Worker* Editorial as 'not worth a day's stoppage in peacetime, let alone in the most critical period of the war'. The paper appealed over the heads of the men to the local leadership. 'The hope of a speedy ending of the lamentable stoppage', it went on, 'rests on the yard leaders. Let them court unpopularity, and ask the strikers to return to work'.[4] The paper refused to print the strike committee's statement, and while Len Powell organised a steady stream of letters from Communist-controlled labour movement bodies urging a return to work, Harry Pollitt sent a personal telegram to every

Communist in the yards calling each striker 'a traitor to his country'. Leaflets appeared calling the stoppage 'a stab in the back for the men of Stalingrad', and calling upon the workers to 'give a courageous lead' by scabbing on the strike, described in a whispering campaign as 'financed by outside bodies'. When the men went back to work, they were told that 'Tyneside shipyard workers can now go forward for the greatest production effort in their history'.

This was a bit out of touch with the men's feelings, to say the least, as was J. R. Campbell's observation that 'a feature of the strike was the lack of hostility between striker and non striker'. For feelings had reached such a pitch that when the local Communist leader attempted to address a meeting he was nearly tossed into the Tyne, and although the men lost the strike they rewarded the Communists by ejecting practically every party member from his position in the elections for shop stewards that followed.[5] The *Daily Worker* attempted to get this revoked by appealing to the higher union committees to reverse the decision:

> 'A well-known Communist has been removed from a yard committee, another from the chairmanship of the Shop Stewards, and some others from departmental positions of shop stewards . . . They cannot be removed from yard committees without the consent of the Confederation or from their Shop Stewards posts without the consent of the District Committee of the Union. It remains for those bodies to support the stewards, who adhered to instructions.'[6]

Throughout, the Communists had been trying to organise scabbing, anti-strike propaganda and a return to work, pretending that the 'strikes would end if inquiry promised'.[7] Crude attempts were made to shame the workers into feeling that they were disloyal, or tools of pro-fascist forces. 'Who gains if production is not kept at its full level?', asked the *Daily Worker*: 'Only Hitler'.[8] It was a bitter taste of things to come.[9]

A year later brought a yet more serious dispute. All through the Spring and Summer of 1943 the Vickers Armstrong shipbuilding works at Barrow were seething with discontent. A report published in August revealed the most unhealthy working conditions:

> 'The yard is grossly overcrowded and conditions are appalling. Men of all trades are crowded together, waiting for each other to finish a job so that they can get on with their own job. There is little or no ventilation, and the fumes and sparks from paint spraying and welding are liable to damage the health of the

workers as well as their clothes . . . a vicious piece work
production bonus system exists which has been in operation since
the last war.'[10]

Not only had the system been in operation for all that time, but the
basic rate for engineers had remained at the same level—46/- for
twenty-nine years! So when the management delayed the
implementation of a new National Tribunal Award (32b) in many
categories of work, the pressure began to build up.

Before the war the *Daily Worker* had made a great show of
defending the Barrow men when they engaged in disputes with the
employers. If they were expecting the same on this occasion they
were in for a shock. The furthest the paper would go to put their case
was refer to the '*alleged* failure to their employers to implement a
national Arbitration Tribunal Award',[11] while advising them to
'return to work and co-operate with their fellows', since 'a
continuation of the strike can only harm the success of the united
national movement'. It was all a regrettable misunderstanding,
explained J. R. Campbell, 'there is no need to strike for an
interpretation of the national award, the Tribunal is going to give
that interpretation in the next two weeks'. This being the case, 'every
Barrow striker must be perfectly clear that he is now being asked to
lose wages for no purpose whatsoever'.[12]

Meanwhile the Lancashire area's Communist Industrial
Organiser, Pat Devine, began to hold meetings outside the yard
entrances pushing the line of production and 'all for the Second
Front', while the two local CP leaders, Whiteside and Wood, tried to
sidetrack the movement and entangle the men in the 'official
negotiating machinery' which had already failed to interpret an
award made as long ago as March. On the 16th April the
Communists got out a circular describing the campaign for higher
wages as 'definitely playing HITLER'S GAME'.[13]

The 21 days' strike notice ran out on September 16th, and the
AEU Committee unanimously agreed to call out their men. All
5,000 engineers instantly struck work, to be followed by some 2,000
electricians, foundrymen, and tradesmen belonging to the eight
other unions that had local branches. Engaging the services of the
Trotskyist Roy Tearse in an advisory capacity, the strike committee
issued a bold appeal for support to the whole engineering industry:

'The workers in other parts of the country have a duty to give
moral and financial support to Barrow. For the first time in years
the Barrow workers have built a real unity in action against the
boss class. Build that unity! Strengthen it! Demonstrate that it has

the support of organised workers from North and South and from coast to coast. For a victory of the Barrow workers is a victory for the workers everywhere.'[14]

This Barrow manifesto marked an important stage in the development of working class opposition to the war. Until that time patriotic feeling still prevented workers on strike in wartime from appealing for outside aid, or generalising their actions, regarding their own disputes as 'special cases' to be properly dealt with by the employers on their own merits. It was a graphic illustration of the rise in working class militancy, with a tremendous degree of solidarity and a high political level.

The Union Executive responded by suspending the whole of the Barrow District Committee of the AEU. Immediately, all the officials of the town's local branch resigned in protest, and were followed by others sympathetic to them in other parts of the country. When the Huddersfield District Committee resigned on September 30th, the AEU dispatched Wal Hannington, their national organiser, with a 'free hand' to reorganise the district. On the 22nd October he visited the Huddersfield No. 2 branch to tell them that he had 'not come to plead with the ex-District Committee members, but to set up a new provisional District Committee'. But the branch endorsed the action of the D.C., and told him in no uncertain terms that it was up to the members to choose who was to serve on their committees, so he may as well go home to London. They were even blunt enough, in their rough Yorkshire way, to rub salt in the wound by reminding him of his history in the union, when he had narrowly escaped expulsion himself.[15] He departed, leaving two stooges in the posts of President and Secretary, with a new District Committee beneath them. But as soon as the January elections came along they were unceremoniously ejected, and all those who had resigned were re-elected to their positions on the District Committee. Hannington went off again, looking distinctly 'down in the dumps'.[16]

Back in Barrow the Youth Committee of the AEU was instructing its apprentices to scab on the men. The YCL's journal, *Challenge*, quoted the Committee's secretary describing how 'Bill Turney, our vice-chairman, showed us that we weren't damaging the men's interests, and although opinion was divided, we won the vote. We stayed at work.' 'The action of the Barrow apprentices during the recent dispute', ran an editorial, 'will be applauded by all young workers. *Challenge*, which is the voice of the young workers, and has always led the fight for their demands congratulates the lads.'[17]

Barrow was, in effect, a one-industry, one-union town, and the strike committee was the same as the AEU district committee. It was a tightly-knit community, the men were rock solid, and they enjoyed the support of the local townsfolk. Against the wall of class feeling, the Communist Party's denunciations became increasingly hysterical. 'Barrow has become a cockpit of Trotskyist agitation' screamed Jack Owen from the pages of the *Daily Worker*.[18] Oblivious to the hatred they were piling up for themselves in the industry, they continued to press the case of the union bureaucracy. 'All who value trade unionism will unfailingly support the leadership of the Amalgamated Engineering Union which is handling the present difficult situation in the great munitions industry with great care and wisdom' was the *Daily Worker*'s comment, since 'to safeguard the union the Executive Council had to suspend the Barrow Committee' because 'disruptors' were delaying the 'united advance towards improved conditions' and 'splitting the unions'.[19]

It was time to call up the professionals to deal with the little town and its stubborn men. Along with the Union's National Organiser, Party member George Crane, came a procession of assorted functionaries—Jack Owen of the *Daily Worker* Editorial Board, Sid Abbot from the Central Committee, and the ETU's National Organiser, Frank Foulkes (of later ballot-rigging fame). A division of labour was decided on, and they set to work with a will.

Owen's job was to spread stories to undermine the men's morale. His opening move was to accuse the strike committee of not calling a proper mass meeting as part of a 'hush-hush' policy to keep the men in the dark.[20] The Committee replied simply by calling his meeting, which voted for the continuation of the strike by 6,000 to 20! His next trick was to relay false information about splits within the strike committee from the Communists on it, to make the men feel that the strike was about to collapse through its leadership coming apart. All he achieved was to get the two Communists expelled from the strike committee, and another two from the committee of the shop stewards. As the official strike bulletin explained it,

'Owing to the present position, in which the Communist Party are attempting to make our struggle into a political issue, and the agreement regarding the giving of information by members of the strike committee (except through official bulletins) has been broken by members of the "Communist" Party, two members of the strike committee, together with two shop stewards, were expelled by a unanimous decision of the shop stewards' meeting.'[21]

His final throw was to insinuate that the council of action was not handing over the monies they had collected in solidarity to the official strike committee.[22]

Sid Abbott's task was to work upon the secretary of the strike committee, Tom Rawlinson, a Communist Party member in arrears with his dues, to get him to resign his position and get the men back to work. He refused, and placed a full record of this manoeuvre before his fellow AEU members.

The line Frank Foulkes chose was to encourage a split of the other trades by securing the withdrawal of the ETU. But from the very first meeting he aroused the hostility of all the strikers. The chairman of the strike committee, AEU council member Tom Trewartha, was moved to issue the following rebuke:

> 'Mr. Foulkes, after having heard your points I am of the opinion that you are a very dishonest person, and come here with one object: to divide the ETU from the AEU. However, you have failed completely. Not only have you failed, but in fact have now cemented the Strike Committee more firmly together than ever before.'[23]

Trewartha's doubts on Foulkes' integrity were to receive more formal sanction in another setting some years later.[24]

Even the International apparatus of the Communists tried to intervene. At that very moment a Soviet Trade Union delegation was on tour in Britain cheerleading the production drive in the factories. Speaking to the Liverpool dockers, the head of the delegates, Mr. Shvernik, described the ports as 'battlefields' in which 'enemy agents sometimes try to assume the character of champions of the workers' interests, calling on them to work less, and pushing them along the path of strike. But to strike now in wartime means to help the enemy'.[25]

The only effect of this anti-strike propaganda was to make the men more determined. Only seven or eight men out of the entire workforce resisted the pickets; but a majority of the Barrow members and sympathisers of the CP resigned, tearing up their subscriptions to the *Daily Worker* along with it. News of the rôle of the Party spread throughout the industry, raising contempt far and wide. An example from a Scottish Shop Stewards' Committee is the following:

> I'm a Communist commando
> howling for a Second Front,
> It really is unkind of you to say it's just a stunt,

Of course it would be barmy
for me to join the army,
When I'm giving all for victory
in an ardent Trotsky hunt.
I'm a patriotic Communist,
on strike I never go.
We must be energetic,
even though the pay is low.
The very name of Barrow
is enough to melt my marrow,
They betrayed dear Ernie Bevin
not to mention Uncle Joe. . .'[26]

Hostility to the Communists even found reflection in the yellow press. 'A factor in the dispute which cannot be disregarded', noted the *Daily Telegraph*, 'is the attitude of the strikers to the Communist Party, several well-known members of which are visiting the town with the object of persuading the men to return to work'.[27] The *Daily Mail* went further, describing Pat Devine as a 'strike-breaker'. But the more the gutter press heaped humiliation on them, the more the Communists crowded forward to demonstrate their respectability. 'When the strike committee expelled Communist members', complained J. R. Campbell, 'it was universally reported that this was for political activity. Thus the uninitiated were led to believe that the Communists were striving to turn an industrial dispute into a political dispute. The fact is that the Communists were expelled because the *Daily Worker* had pointed to the machinations of the Trotskyists behind the scenes and their hopes of extending the Barrow dispute to other parts of the country'.[28]

Even Bevin, with an eye on the future, was too astute a politician to let slip an opportunity to make political capital out of their unpopularity. While they were doing his work for him he poured out his scorn in a speech made at Farnworth in Lancashire:

'We have had the Communists seeking power for a long time, and now we get another sect trying to kill the Communists. One flea biting another flea. Don't let them both bite you.'[29]

A long letter of reply came from William Rust, Editor of the *Daily Worker*, setting out in detail all the contributions of his party to the success of Bevin's policies, from the Wigan Miners' Organiser Jim Hammond ('who set himself against strikes, as all Communists do') to the efforts of George Crane in Barrow. It revealed the ambitions of the Communists to replace Labour at the head of the working class at the end of the war:

'A statesman, and trade union leaders, must also be a good nurseryman. He must plant and carefully tend young trees, otherwise when the old ones fall there will be none to replace them.'

It ended on an undignified note:

'The handling of the Barrow strike has not been an easy job for the *Daily Worker*. I have had many headaches over it. We intensely sympathise with the Barrow men and their grievances which must be righted. But we know that they took the wrong path, that the strike action was harmful to the war effort and to the AEU.'[30]

But the Barrow strikers resisted the pressure of the employers, the mass media, and their labour agents alike. The whole community was behind them, and such was the strength of their position, that when Sir Charles Craven asked to speak with the strike committee, they refused to meet him on his own ground and compelled him to attend them instead! After eighteen days the management were forced to cave in and sue for terms. Even though the National Tribunal had awarded no increase at all to time and a half men, very little to the low paid, and but seven shillings a week to those on higher rates, increases were won ranging from three-and-fourpence-farthing to 33 shillings after the national machinery had been tried for six and a half months with no result at all.

If past experience taught the management to accept their defeat with a good grace, the same could not be said for the Communist Party. 'Given the opportunity by the employers', noted the *Daily Worker* ingenuously, 'we are certain that they will make up the lost output and show that they stand four square with the main body of the British workers'.[31] Pollitt did his best to glean some advantage by blaming the strike on the 'widespread suspicion' of the workers at the 'prolonged delay in organising the Second Front', according to him being utilised 'by employers and by reactionary Trotskyist political forces'.[32] Whether the strikers agreed that their dispute was carried on to assist Communist propaganda is not recorded. As for Devine himself, an article he wrote to lick his wounds called 'Never Again' showed that, like the Bourbons, he had learned nothing and forgotten everything:

'But the strike could have been prevented, and an effective remedying of grievances secured if the Barrow trade unionists had found the ways and means of utilising the machinery of their unions and brought strong pressure to bear on the government.'

The whole regrettable experience was described as justifying the Communists in 'leading the workers to secure a remedy of their grievances without strikes, and must ever keep the great issues of the war before them'.[33]

Disturbances in the engineering industry were eclipsed in both scale and frequency by those in mining towards the end of the war. Here it was a case of a run-down sector, with a tired and aging workforce labouring in terrible conditions at unattractive rates of pay. True to their traditional attitudes, the mineowners were under-investing and over-exploiting, and were even taking advantage of the guaranteed market by deliberately working poor seams. When France fell they had even closed some mines, anticipating a loss of markets, whilst keeping back the best for extra profiteering after the end of the war. After the war had ended, few even among the business classes shed a tear at the passing of the pits into public ownership, so selfish and short-sighted the employers proved to be. Nationalisation came not a moment too soon; by 1945 the industry was on the edge of collapse.

When the war broke out, opposition to the government, and resentment at the bad conditions in the pits, died down for a while with that usual burst of patriotism that accompanies the beginning of war. 1940 registered the lowest number of workdays lost in any time since statistics had been taken. But as war dragged into its third year the sheer exploitation of an old and tired workforce produced a steady rise in strikes and absenteeism. Even the rallying of the Communist Party to the 'National Front' after June, 1941 could make no impact on this militancy, loyal though the miners continued to be to their old traditions, and just as reluctant to use the strike weapon after the terrible defeat of 1926. When the rise in industrial militancy led to a loss in working days in all industries in 1944 that was the highest on record since 1932, we must remember that the coal industry alone was responsible for two-thirds of that, and half the workdays lost in the previous year.[34]

The drop in production was absolutely catastrophic for the manufacture of steel and hence to the further prosecution of the war. An estimate made in 1944 held that production was 450,000 tons a week less than current requirements, and that total annual production had fallen to between 30 and 40 million tons less than before the war.[35] The weekly output per man dropped from 5.81 to 5.3 tons between 1939 and 1943.

The causes went back a generation. Since the General Strike the miners had sustained defeat after defeat, and the whole industry had gone into a pronounced decline. Wage-rates had been alarmingly depressed, and there was hardly a coalfield that did not suffer from chronic under-investment. Not surprisingly, young men were just not going into the pits, and were leaving the mining areas for more rewarding pay elsewhere, especially in engineering. By 1942, the Miners' Federation was estimating that 40% of the workforce was over the age of 40,[36] a real danger signal in an industry that depended above all on sheer physical labour. The poor wage rates in turn prevented new blood from coming in; one survey showed that in 10 of the 16 main districts boys were getting a mere 10 shillings a shift, while attendance at a government training centre would rapidly produce an engineer's wage of between £3 0s. 6d. and £3 10s. 6d. a week![37]

The traditional market mechanisms of unemployment or high wages were not available to attract labour to the pits, so the government resorted to measures of compulsion. The Essential Work Order of May 15, 1940, and the Emergency Powers (Defence) Act of May 22, 1940, tied colliers to the job, practically as serfs. If these did not suffice, there was always more longstanding legislation, such as the Trades Disputes Act of 1927, or even the Coal Mines Act of 1911. 'They were such powers', wrote a Communist miners' historian later, 'as no government, democratic or despotic, modern or feudal, had ever possessed in this country. *There began to be keen disappointment that these powers were not used*'.[38]

The government did use its powers, to their satisfaction if not to his. A thousand miners on strike at Betteshanger in Kent were given the option of £1 fine or 14 days' prison and three of their branch officers were jailed. Miners at Valleyfield in Fife, and Cortonwood and Hatfield Main near Doncaster were fined for illegal strikes, and at the Tareni colliery in South Wales strikers were imprisoned for a month. By March 1945 no less than 18,436 had been punished under the Essential Works Order for lateness or absenteeism, and 1,323 of them had been jailed. Miners accounted for a horrifying number of these. Yet not a single one of the 127 employers prosecuted for infraction of the labour laws in the whole of industry up to February 1944 had ever seen the inside of a prison.[40]

Other measures were not neglected. 'In the last six months', Bevin informed the House of Commons in June, 1942, 'I have transferred, at great loss of wages to themselves, over 30,000 men from munitions factories to the mines'.[41] Even this was felt to be inadequate, and after the Cortonwood strike he brought in Regulation 1AA, by which instigating a strike or stoppage in wartime essential work became an offence in itself. Fortunately, the storm of opposition it raised from the miners, and even in Parliament, prevented it from being implemented, but the sheer volume of repressive legislation as a whole rendered it redundant anyway. As F. S. Cocks MP explained to the House of Commons, 'if you abolished the Essential Work Order, half the men in the pits would leave the industry tomorrow of their own voluntary accord'.[42] Despite this enormous apparatus of power ranged against them—and the chorus of 'public opinion' that accompanied it—the miners fought back with stubborn courage. But the Communist Party ranged itself alongside the employers. Between 1942 and 1943 all eleven pits in the Doncaster area were involved in strikes over wage cutting: and at the Cortonwood pit near Wombwell, 1,500 miners were out during December 1941 and May 1942 over an agreement signed by Joe Hall, the leader of the Yorkshire miners, which cut fillers' rates by from 1/7d. to 1/3d. per ton (a loss to the weekly wage packet of between 30 shillings and £3). Despite the fact that the men had not been consulted over the new rates—or even informed about them in many cases—the *Daily Worker* worked itself up into a state of moral outrage because 'The Independent Labour Party and the Trotskyists in complete indifference to the fuel crisis, have been engaged in persuading the miners to remain on strike—against an agreement signed by their own officials!'[43] Angered at the support of the Trotskyists for the men's case, T. Dagenham, a Communist Party member, managed to get a resolution through the council of the Yorkshire miners authorising the union's officials 'to take legal advice as to what action, if any, can be taken in regard to the articles which are continually appearing in *Socialist Appeal*.[44] (When the *Daily Worker* reported this it omitted to say that the resolution had been put down by one of its own supporters.)[45] Up in Scotland, where the Communists enjoyed more support, the situation was worse. In February 1943, 1,100 men struck work at the Bowhill colliery in Fife against a proposed reduction in wages of twopence a ton, in the teeth of threats that they would be fired and then be made liable for military service. Gallacher wrote in the *Glasgow Evening Times* (27th February, 1943) trying the old device of entangling the men in the official channels:

'I want to see every injustice remedied, but in the present circumstances to strike is not the way to do it. It can be done by utilising fully the trade union machinery and the existing agreements arrived at between the trades unions, the employers, and the Government.'

It took his efforts, and those of Abe Moffat, Communist member of the Executive of the Scottish Miners' Federation, to get the strikers to accept a cut of one penny per ton.[46] Only a month afterwards Moffat was at work trying to stop solidarity action spreading to other pits from the Valleyfield colliery, where 32 men had been fined for striking without giving the statutory 21 days' notice against an attempt of the employers to cut the number of men working on the face.[47] When miners from the Blairhall pit, also in Fife, landed in jail for a similar action, the strike was ended when the President of their branch of the union, a leading Communist, went behind their backs and paid the fines that they had refused to produce.[48] And along with it came smears against the men and any Socialists who spoke for them. One leaflet under the title of *Poison in the Coalfields*, called on the miners not to 'scab on the Red Army and the miners of France and Belgium by disorganising coal production without which no armed struggle against Hitler can take place'.[49] Of the Stalinist leaders in Scotland, Harry McShane in particular was to the fore in this witchhunting,[50] falsely accusing supporters of the *Militant Scottish Miner* of chairing meetings for the Duke of Bedford, described as a pacifist and pro-Nazi,[51] and Abe Moffat went on record in the bourgeois press against what he described as a 'deliberate planned attempt to destroy the trade union'.[52]

The other coalfield where the Communist Party was deeply rooted was South Wales, and here Arthur Horner was the main mover inside the official apparatus of the union. In June 1943 men working in difficult conditions at the Tareni colliery were jailed for refusing to pay a fine of £20 for 'impeding production'. When five neighbouring pits came out in sympathy, Horner worked with might and main to stop the spread of the strike.[53] A worse case came from the Gelliceidrim pit, where miners halted work when the owners refused to undertake the customary tests in an area notoriously subject to past flooding. When the employers were finally forced to make the tests on the eighteenth day (until then they had merely produced a map made before a previous flood-in), Horner agreed with the men about the need for the tests, but told them that they couldn't claim the guaranteed wage for the period in which they had refused to work the area![54]

Horner also played a crucial rôle in getting the South Wales miners to accept the belated 'Porter Award' of February 1944. It caused widespread uproar by fixing the minimum wage so low that it was beneath what some men were getting already—so they gained not a penny. Skilled men and piece workers not only did not make any gains, but some even suffered reductions. For though surface pay was raised by one shilling, 1/6d. was levied on the concessionary coal used by the miners for domestic purposes, amounting to a cut in wages! Soon 100,000 were out in South Wales, and another 80,000 in South Yorkshire. The Communists' attempt to stem this enormous explosion of miners' anger was like so much howling into the wind. 'It is impossible', cried a *Daily Worker* Editorial, 'on the eve of the Second Front to tolerate a stoppage in its war factories, due to the continuance of the coal strike in Yorkshire. We urge the Yorkshire miners to heed Mr. Bevin's warning and return immediately. . . This question can only be discussed when Yorkshire returns.'[55] In a union in which the problem of separate areas with varying rates of pay has played such a destructive role, the Communists worked hard to isolate the Yorkshiremen by playing on the differences. 'It is not explained that this is a claim for special privilege for Yorkshire in relation to other districts', they complained, and went on to insult the Yorks Federation as a 'puerile union leadership which has never faced the bosses or the government'.[56] When these men went back to work, their feelings towards the Communist Party can well be imagined—which might explain why they have never been able to make any electoral inroads into this, the most solid block of Labour supporters in the country.

Whilst the colliers were defending themselves, the government moved on to new instruments of compulsion to get other parts of the workforce into the mines. In July 1943 Bevin announced his Coalmining (Compulsory Recruitment) Bill, which was to become law on December 2nd. This was the famous 'Bevin Ballot Scheme', in which young people—many of them engineering apprentices— were removed from their jobs and put to work in the pits at lower rates of pay, sent all over the country, and even billetted on private households. Bevin was careful to secure the full co-operation of the Miners' Federation in advance by announcing his plan to their annual conference. He also received the (unsolicited) support of the Communists. 'We have to be prepared to adopt speedily any and every measure to increase the production of coal', argued the *Daily Worker*: 'Our youth are being sent into the industry to serve the needs of their country, not to increase the profits of the mineowners.'[58]

It was bound to cause trouble, for the apprentices bitterly resented it, and even some miners were suspicious that it would mean skilled men losing bonus payments when put to work along with unskilled youths. Naturally though, the miners did not feel the apprentices' injustice strongly—they were already having to labour down the pits anyway, and felt that those in outside industries were relatively privileged (which was indeed the case). The apprentices would have been totally isolated from the miners if they had not been well advised by the Militant Workers' Federation, the industrial

organisation of the Trotskyists, to include in their demands the
nationalisation of the mines, and to agree to drop their objections to
going down them if this were done.

Rumbles of discontent began with a strike at Askern, near
Pontefract, and demonstrations in Coventry and Swinton. Then in
March 1944, 5,000 apprentices struck on Tyneside, a stoppage which
spread to the Wear and the Tees, and soon took on the complexion of
a national apprentices' strike when they were joined by 20,000 on the
Clyde and 1,000 in Huddersfield. The strike leader, Bill Davy, later
became a Trotskyist and was assisted at the time by the Trotskyist
Workers' International League (in the process of becoming the
Revolutionary Communist Party)—in particular by Heaton Lee and
Ann Keen on the spot, and Roy Tearse, Secretary of the Militant
Workers' Federation. The action combined the two things that the
Communists loathed the most—left-wing opposition and striking in
wartime—and they used all their influence to break it up. Firstly,
they tried to divide off the apprentices on the Tyne from those under
their own influence on Teeside.[59] When they found out how solid the
lads were, they next tried to act as industrial police to ferret out men
who had left the pits and send them down instead. A Statement put
out by the North Eastern District of the Communist Party ran:

'The Tyne District Committee of the Amalgamated Engineering
Union (AEU) has completed a list of ex-miners working in the
factories and shipyards. It has submitted this list to the Ministry of
Labour for appropriate action. . .

A resolution calling for this step to be taken was moved by a
Communist at the last Quarterly Meeting of the Shop
Stewards'.[60]

Finally, the authorities moved in and arrested the Trotskyists, Roy
Tearse, Heaton Lee and Ann Keen, and later Jock Haston. While the
trial—and the appeal that followed—were still taking place, the
Communists applauded vigorously, smearing the accused by leaflet
and in the party press, and trying to demoralise the apprentices by
claiming that they were being manipulated by pro-Nazi Trotskyists
behind the scenes.[61] As the law stood, it amounted to interference
with the course of justice, though of course no prosecution was
mounted against the Communists for doing it. Disgust at the
treatment of the accused was so universal, that Jimmie Maxton put
himself at the head of the defence committee, and Bevan spoke up for
them in the House of Commons:

'The alleged Trotskyites had been kept in remand for twenty-one days and tried in camera, the explanation of the secret trial being that the police had not been able to complete their investigations into their alleged offences. The newspapers had piled up public hatred against them and committed contempt of court on a fantastic scale. Yet no action was taken by 'this venal Government' to protect them in any way'. (M. Foot, *Aneurin Bevan*, November 1966 edition, p. 392.)

But the only complaint of the Communists was that the trial had taken place under the Trades Disputes Act of 1927—universally regarded as anti-Labour legislation for as long as it remained on the statute book—when the prosecution could just as well have taken place under other laws instead![62]

By now the Communist Party, at its furthest rightward point of evolution, should have discovered that it was riding a whirlwind. The sigh of relief with which people were greeting the end of the war was also a judgement on the old order that had produced it. Strikes died down for a while now—one last heave and it was all over—but a deep-going radicalisation spread throughout the working class, upwards through the middle strata, and into the ranks of the armed forces. Already during the war the forces' parliament in Cairo had shown a tremendous shift to the left among the soldiers, with support for strikes and democratic liberties in wartime. as being in their opinion for what they were fighting. The Eighth Army Signals debated and rejected a resolution putting forward the usual establishment and Communist line that

'Strikes are harmful to our National Interests abroad, for they create the impression of National Disunity and diversion from the main purpose of our war effort. They make Russia suspicious of our sincerity and give Germany material for injurious propaganda in occupied and neutral countries.'[63]

At the same time 82 soldiers petitioned the Home Secretary for the release of the imprisoned Trotskyists, identifying with the struggle of the miners 'to maintain workers' rights', blaming the government, and calling for nationalisation.[64]

The movement to the left among the forces—conscripted workers in uniform without rights of their own, after all—was a reflection of the state of the rest of the country. Sooner or later the strike wave was bound to reflect itself in the traditional political institutions of the working class. That gradual increase in the fortunes of the Labour Party from the defeat of 1931, interrupted by the war for a brief time, now swelled into a mighty movement. And the Communists were against it.

Footnotes

1 Jack Tanner, Speech to the 45th Annual Conference of the Labour Party, Bournemouth, June, 1946—official report, p. 173.
2 'CP Policy in the Royal Ordnance Factories', in *Socialist Appeal*, vol. iv, no. 9, June, 1942, p. 4.
3 *Daily Worker*, 7th September, 1942; *cf. Socialist Appeal*, vol. iv, no. 12, September, 1942, p. 2.
4 'End This Strike', in the *Daily Worker*, 6th October, 1942.
5 Jock Haston, 'Tyne Workers Close Ranks', in *Socialist Appeal*, vol. v, no. 2, November, 1942; Don McGregor, *Shop Stewards Pamphlet*, no. 1, December, 1942, p. 5.
6 'Tyne Stewards: Will Unions Act?' in the *Daily Worker*, 15th October, 1942.
7 Ben Francis, 'Strikes Would End if Inquiry Promised', in the *Daily Worker*, 10th October, 1942.
8 Editorial, 'Who Gains?' in the *Daily Worker*, 20th October, 1942.
9 For the above account, *cf.* the references in notes 4-8 above, and the following issues of the *Daily Worker*, 10th September ('Peace Moves in Tyneside Dispute'), 12th September ('Tyne Shipyard Settlement') 13th October ('Tyneside Strikers Go Back'), etc.
10 M. Orton, 'Chaos at Vickers Armstrong', in *Socialist Appeal*, vol. iv, no. 11, August 1942, p. 2.
11 'Barrow Strike Goes on', in the *Daily Worker*, 22nd September, 1943 (our emphasis).
12 J. R. Campbell, 'Out to Break the AEU', in the *Daily Worker*, 17th September, 1943.
13 Jock Haston, 'Barrow Engineers Out: 100% Solidarity Among Other Trades', in *Socialist Appeal*, vol. v, no. 19, mid-September, 1943, p. 4.
14 Jock Haston, *Barrow Workers Fight for Living Wage*, leaflet supplement to *Socialist Appeal*, p. 4.
15 'The Man Who Went to Huddersfield: Barrow Has Created Problems for AEU', unsigned article in the *New Leader*, vol. xxxv, no. 35, 6th November, 1943.
16 *New Leader*, vol. xxxv, no. 44, 8th January, 1944.
17 *Challenge*, 9th October, 1943.
18 Jack Owen, 'Trotskyists Trying to Prolong the Barrow Strike', in the *Daily Worker*, 27th September, 1943.
19 'The AEU', in the *Daily Worker*, 2nd October, 1943.
20 *cf.* note 18 above.
21 Official Bulletin quote by Haston, 'Lessons of the Barrow Strike', in *Socialist Appeal*, vol. v, no. 20, October, 1943, p. 4.
22 Jack Owen, 'Barrow Strike Confusion', in the *Daily Worker*, 12th October, 1943.
23 Quoted by Jimmy Deane, 'Barrow Workers Victorious', in *Socialist Appeal*', vol. v, no. 20, October, 1943, p. 4.
24 i.e. the ETU Ballott-Rigging Scandal.
25 'Your Ports Are Battlefields Shvernik Tells Dockers', in the *Daily Worker*, 8th October, 1943.
26 'Davidovitch', in *The Rangefinder*, Journal of the Barr Strouds' Shop Stewards, as quoted by the supplement to *Socialist Appeal*, vol. v, no. 24, mid-December, 1943, p. 2.

27 Quoted by Walter Holmes, 'Strike Breaker', in the *Daily Worker*, 8th October, 1943.
28 J. R. Campbell, 'Barrow and the Press', in the *Daily Worker*, 8th October, 1943.
29 *Daily Herald*, 2nd October, 1943; *cf.* W. Rust, 'An Open Letter to the Minister of Labour from the Editor', in the *Daily Worker*, 5th October, 1943.
30 W. Rust, 'An Open Letter to the Minister of Labour from the Editor', in the *Daily Worker*, 5th October, 1943.
31 'After the Strike', in the *Daily Worker*, 5th October, 1943.
32 H. Pollitt, 'Industrial Unrest and its Causes', in *World News and Views*, vol. xxiii, no. 41, 9th October, 1943, p. 321.
33 Pat Devine, 'Never Again', in the *Daily Worker*, 11th October, 1943, p. 2.
34 The following table of workdays lost in disputes over this period may prove useful, adapted from those given in M. Heineman, *Britain's Coal; A Study of the Mining Crisis*, London, 1944, p. 28, and R. Page Arnot, *The Miners in Crisis and War*, London, 1961, p. 396:

Year	No. of disputes	No. of workers involved	No. of workdays lost
1942	526	252,000	840,000
1943	835	295,000	890,000
1944	1,253	586,000	2,480,000

35 Heineman, *op. cit.*, p. 19.
36 Statement of June 8th, 1942, quoted in R. Page Arnot, *op. cit.*, p. 347.
37 Heineman, *op. cit.*, p. 46.
38 R. Page Arnot, *op. cit.*, p. 311 (our emphasis).
39 J. Gale, 'The Working Class Fights Back', in *Workers Press*, 10th November, 1975, p. 4.
40 'Workers Jailed, Bosses Get Off', in the *Daily Worker*, 21st April, 1944, p. 4
41 Quoted in Heineman, *op. cit.*, p, 45, and Arnot, p. 345.
42 Quoted in Arnot, p. 386.
43 *Daily Worker*, 29th December, 1942.
44 'Open Letter to the Yorkshire Miners', in *Socialist Appeal*, vol. v, no. 4, January, 1943. *Cf.* also no. 5, February, 1943.
45 *Cf.* Above, n. 43.
46 Jack Gale, 'Miners in the War', in *Workers Press*, 24th August, 1972. *Cf.* 'The Working Class Fights Back', in *Workers Press*, 10th November, 1975. The authors are much indebted to this study, based upon the relevant issues of *Socialist Appeal*, for what follows.
47 *Ibid*
48 Brannan, *The Miners' Next Step*, ILP pamphlet, no date, p. 4; 'Fife Dispute' in the *Militant*, new series no. 10, September, 1942.
49 'Once Again the Communist Party', in the *Militant Scottish Miner*, new series no. 15, May 1943, p. 1.
50 A fact curiously omitted from his autobiography recently published by Pluto Press—H. McShane and Joan Smith, *No Mean Fighter*, London, 1978.
51 *Daily Worker*, 1st October, 1943. *Cf.* G. Russell, 'Union Circular or CP Slander Sheet?', in *The Militant Miner*, new series no. 27, August, 1944.
52 *Evening Citizen*, 29th September, 1943.
53 *Cf.* under n. 46 above.
54 '400 Welsh Miners Strike', in *Socialist Appeal*, vol. vi, no. 7, November, 1944.
55 Editorial, 'Go Back', in the *Daily Worker*, 5th April, 1944.
56 *Daily Worker*, 8th April, 1944.

57 Arnot, *op. cit*, p. 378.

58 *Daily Worker*, 21st July, 1943.

59 'Daily Worker Reporter', 'Teesside Apprentices Say: Strike Cannot Achieve its Object', in the *Daily Worker*, 1st April, 1944.

60 Quoted in J. Gale, 'The Working Class Fights Back', in *Workers Press*, 10th November, 1975.

61 J. R. Campbell, 'Lads Duped to Aid Trotskyist and ILP Anti-War Propaganda', in · the *Daily Worker*, 4th April, 1944: 'Trotskyist Saboteurs', in the *Daily Worker*, 10th April, 1944 (reproduced separately for distribution as a leaflet).

62 'Trotskyism: A Warning: Effort to Confuse the Public', Statement of the EC of the CPGB, in the *Daily Worker*, 19th April, 1944; 'Trotskyist Organisation', statement of the EC of the CPGB, in *World News and Views*, vol. xxiv, no. 17, 22nd April, 1944, p. 130; D. N. Pritt, 'No Strike Order—Sinister in its Vagueness', in the *Daily Worker*, 26th April, 1944.

63 *Socialist Appeal*, vol. v, no. 23, mid-May, 1944.

64 *Ibid.*

Chapter Eight

The March Past, 1945

The immense swing to the left in Britain was the local reflection of a worldwide process. In China, Albania, Yugoslavia and Greece partizans led by Communists had liberated large areas of their countries from the enemy, arms in hand, before the axis powers had surrendered. In Italy and France the Communists had emerged at the head of the resistance and the largest parties of the labour movement in their respective countries, not only facing regimes that were utterly discredited, but ready, with their own apparatus of armed power, to take over if they so wished. A wave of enthusiasm for the Red Army was sweeping across the world, as it advanced as far west as Torgau in Germany. Apart from these visible signs of a leftward drift, a feeling common to all peoples expressed the wish for a new world. For whilst war—'the locomotive of history'—kills, destroys and maims, it also cleans away the outworn lumber of the centuries, overturns prejudices, and obliterates regimes that have long outlived their usefulness. In the case of the axis powers the war had destroyed them in a physical sense; but even among the victors, workers, peasants and soldiers felt that their sacrifices would have been in vain if the world order that had caused the war should remain to cause more trouble in the future. A real revolutionary crisis had matured— not, of course, of the same depth in all countries—just as had happened at the end of the First World War.

A central part in the stabilisation of the situation was played by the Soviet Union, and through it the Communist parties of the world. In Eastern Europe the Russian Army put mixed regimes in control of the newly liberated countries, including (along with their own appointees) the most reactionary politicians of the old order— monarchists in Romania, Horthyite dictators in Hungary, and bourgeois 'nationalist' politicians all over the place. In Bulgaria they went in for a mass purge and suppression of the Anarchist movement, using the repressive organs of the old state; and when their army crossed the Czechoslovak border, and sympathisers appeared in the streets wearing the red star, they gave orders that they were to be shot. In Yugoslavia and China they put pressure on the native Communists to go into coalition with the most discredited pre-war politicians; and Russia stood aside while the British army in Greece smashed the Communist-led partizans to restore the monarchy.

Where the direct arm of Stalin could not extend, the Communist parties filled the same rôle. Communists entered coalition governments in France and Italy, where they disarmed the partizans, reconstructed the old state, and became the most vicious strike-breakers and supporters of colonial war. 'We are not even interested in the question of a 40-hour week', said the Secretary of the French Communist Party, even before coming to power: 'as far as we are concerned, the workers will work sixty hours weekly if it is necessary for the rehabilitation of France'.[1] Their paper *L'Humanité* even defined strikes as 'the weapon of the trusts';[2] and Communist deputies voted for the colonial war in Vietnam against their own comrades with unseemly enthusiasm. In America, the Communist Party came out with the theory that capitalism there had not exhausted its expansive potential, and true to political logic, went into dissolution and formed a 'political association' instead.

It was counter-revolution on a world scale. As Frank Allaun, resigning from the Communist Party at this time, put it,

> 'He (i.e. Earl Browder) didn't merely say that 'the American people are not ripe for Socialism' (in which case the American CP has been wrong for the last 20 years); or that collaboration with the biggest capitalists should continue after the war 'for a long period of years' (not just until the Roosevelt election); but that there should be no violent social change in Europe as that would spoil the market for American manufacturers' exports! In answer to questions on his speech he says, 'Millions in Europe will be engaged in the mighty task of reconstruction under broadly democratic governments within the framework of the capitalist system'.
>
> Confusion of the fact that the CP was not going to fight for a Socialist Europe was given in a recent 3-lesson course for tutors, by Robson. Yet neither tutors nor members have ever been consulted on this unwarranted assumption. . .
>
> If all this is a Socialist policy, I am afraid I am too dull to understand it, and that there will be other members of the CP, and the general public, equally stupid.'[3]

But neither the general public, nor the labour movement failed to get the message: as Herbert Morrison remarked to the 1946 conference of the Labour Party, 'They are not a Party of the Left as far as I can see. They are not here, they are not abroad.'[4]

The British Communist Party was no exception to the rule, laid down as it was in Moscow. For the more the masses expressed their hostility to the old Tory politicians, the more Communists and their fellow-travellers moved closer to them. When Churchill first began to lose his popularity, D. N. Pritt dealt with it in his diary:

I gather from a good many people that Churchill's name is at any rate at present mud in the Army and the factories and generally elsewhere. I am not sure that they know clearly what they want to do when they have got rid of him, but they want to get rid of him . . .

It seems to me that the proper line for me to take is still to say "we must have Churchill as Prime Minister", but to criticise him fairly sharply for mismanaging the government, press him more strongly than ever to get rid of a good stock of his colleagues but above all to press him to work in the closest co-operation with the Soviet and Chinese peoples, get into personal touch with them, fight in accordance with their strategy, and aim at victory in 1942'. (*Diary*, 17th February, 1942.)[5]

So while a deep-going ferment was going on among the rank-and-file of the Labour Party and trade unions, expressed in the desire to break the coalition and run alone for government in the following elections, the Communists were still eaten up with enthusiasm for the coalition government. As Pollitt himself expressed it,

'Its experience in working with such allies during the war—even when an out-of-date Parliament has given the Tory Party the dominant positions in the National government and a majority in Parliament—has proved to be in the best interests of the working class.'[6]

Worse still, Communists were forgetting completely the language of class struggle at the precise moment the workers outside were relearning it. 'The difficulty of those who forever shout about "what's become of the class struggle"', complained Pollitt, 'is that they always see it where it does not exist, and miss it where it does exist in its most decisive form.'[7]

Its 'most decisive form' was not, as far as Pollitt was concerned, at the level of state power. As far as he knew, only 'the so-called "Left" of the Labour Movement—those without mass influence or serious responsibility' had openly described his policy as 'a betrayal of Socialism'.[8] He did not know that huge numbers of workers were shortly to share this opinion—and show who was really 'without mass influence or serious responsibility' into the bargain. Anyway, he refused to follow them, for 'to take refuge in passivity or loud-sounding "revolutionary" phrases, because of the very real difficulties that exist, would be a retreat from serious political leadership, and a defeatist under-estimation of the strength of the organised working class'.[9] He saw a new community of interests between the classes, overriding the tired philosophy of class war. 'The preservation of peace', he wrote, 'is in the interests of the majority of the *people*, not only of the middle classes and the workers, but sections of the capitalist class who are increasingly beginning to understand this'.[10] The implication was that the capitalists had mistakenly plunged the world into war against their own interests, and after desolating large tracts of it had now suddenly realised how wrong it all was. The Communist Party, for its part, was not going to fight the class struggle in any form, but was going to work for the damping down of the wave of radicalisation and the continuation of the wartime coalition. Communists campaigned on behalf of Tories against Common Wealth at by-elections,[11] and only three months before the Labour Conference decided to break the coalition and aim for a Labour majority Pollitt was still writing:

> 'There are certain sections in the Labour movement who encourage this criticism and defeatism, who demand that Labour should now leave the Government, and who can see nothing in its record except that Labour members have been "tricked" by more cunning Tories. According to them, this is the only way to protect the interests of the working class and to advance to Socialism. It has to be clearly understood that this is not a revolutionary viewpoint, though nobody talks more about revolution than those who advocate this policy.'[12]

On this basis the Communists began again one of their 'unity' offensives against the Labour Party. But on two occasions when they pressed it they got the quick reply that 'it would serve no useful purpose'; and a conference called to support the continuation of the coalition in London on the 2nd September, 1944, had a ban imposed upon Labour participation by the National Executive.[13] Pollitt even tried to revive his old scheme of selecting the Labour Party's candidates for it,[14] when he advised that to gain 'the support of all that is best in the country, irrespective of their class or social connections' it was the Communist view that 'on the question of candidates, we consider that the aim should be to get the very best that each party has within its ranks.'[15]

On the 7th October, 1944, the NEC issued its policy document entitled *Labour and the General Election*, which included the statement that

'When it is time for the House of Commons to be renewed the Labour Party, proud of the share it has taken in winning the War and preparing for the Peace, will go before the country with a practical policy based upon the Socialist principles in which it believes and will invite the electors to return a majority pledged to support the Labour Government to implement that policy.'[16]

When the annual conference convened to ratify it at Westminster two months later, there was a campaign mounted by the Communists and their allies to reverse it, which took the form of attempting to refer back the above paragraph in the interests of 'progressive unity'. They came in for some withering criticism, not only on the grounds of class feeling, but for falling short even of the principles of bourgeois democracy. This was the view defended by Woodburn, sitting MP for Clackmannan and East Stirling:

'The plea for unity is put forward on the grounds that it is going to bring a majority at the Election—that is, on the grounds of expediency. We are asked to sell seats to the Liberals, to Common Wealth and to the Communists. But in a democracy it is not in our power to sell seats; it is the electors' right to chose who is to be the Member, not for us to decide who goes into Parliament. The Labour Party, on principle, objects to rich men's parties, because a party that is willing to be subsidised by rich men, when the rich men stop those subsidies, is apt to be ready to sell itself to the next highest bidder. We cannot compromise with a body of that kind . . . They (i.e. the CP) are putting up candidates all over the place to see that some Tory or Liberal gets back to Parliament. That is a new form of unity to me . . .'[17]

The amendment was defeated with a huge majority. But Communists opened up another campaign to reverse the decision before a general election could be called, and it was too late. Here they were most unfortunate, for their intended allies, the Tories, cut short the time available by springing a snap election themselves. By

now coalition was a fixed idea for the Communists, and affected
their thinking to an incredible degree. At the same time as they were
disseminating defeatist propaganda throughout the whole country,
that Labour had no chance of winning the election outright, they had
the nerve to describe the Labour leaders (whose feel for the
movement was more sensitive than their own) of being defeatist!:

'We want to end the spirit of defeatism and lack of confidence
which is still often shown within the Labour movement, the spirit
which denies the power and capacity of the Labour movement to
win the majority of the people and build up national unity around
its leadership; the paralysing fear and distrust which sees Toryism
as always dominant and can only conceive of Labour entering into
a coalition as a junior partner of Toryism'.[18]

But only months earlier their own literature had been justifying
the coalition on the grounds that 'the Labour movement is not yet
strong enough to lead the nation'![19]   Of course the Communists'
opposition to the break-up of the National Government and
Labour's decision to go it alone had nothing to do with either
assessment based upon the domestic situation. Insensitive to the
stirrings of a mighty movement beneath them, their eyes were
firmly fixed on the international plane, where Churchill, Roosevelt
and Stalin were disposing the fate of the world at their summit
meetings.

Out of these discussions, the Communists selected the Yalta
Conference as a model for arranging the post-war world, and
ascribed quite extraordinary importance to it. Apart from the worldwide scope of its decisions, what attracted them most was the spirit
of general harmony between the Soviet Union and the two Western
states, the harbinger of peace, so they hoped, on a long-term basis. It
was also the guarantor of the special privileges enjoyed by the
Communists, for the end of the war found them firmly ensconced in
governmental positions in most of western Europe. On the spirit of
Yalta were based the British Communist Party's hopes of a dip into
the trough—and who knows, it could even amount to a cabinet
position, or at least a few seats in parliament—no more than they
deserved for their immense sacrifices 'in the national interest'.

Support for the Yalta Accords also fitted in neatly with the policy
of a broad coalition after the war that would include members of all
parties—all, that is, except the ILP, which had not conformed to the
'national interest', for when the Yalta agreement was brought to
Parliament for ratification in February and March 1945, the ILP
alone voted against it. The only accommodation to the mass mood

that the CP were willing to make was that Labour should replace the Conservatives as the main party of this post-war coalition. 'We shall do all in our power', Pollitt promised, 'to obtain such forms of electoral unity as can ensure the defeat of the Tory Party at the coming General Election, and the formation of a new type of National Government based on a Labour and Progressive majority.'[20] But who, (apart from the Communists themselves) were these 'Progressives'? None other than the Tory and Liberal supporters of the Yalta Accords! For Pollitt thought that the Labour leaders had not reckoned with 'the enormous change which is taking place in the outlook of the people, the' differentiation within the ranks of Toryism and the opportunity opening out to Labour to build and lead the new governmental combination.'[21] For though the CP defined their policy as 'a ceaseless political struggle against all the reactionary sections of the capitalist class and the enemies of the decisions of the Crimea Conference',[22] the fact remained that no section of the Tories of any importance had gone on record against Yalta—only the ILP!

It was a subtle policy indeed—far too subtle for millions of working men and soldiers to understand, for they only saw against them the parties of wealth and privilege, presided over by their old enemy, the warmonger Churchill. But this was proof to the CP of how 'backward' the British working class were. 'In our country', wrote Peter Kerrigan, 'the understanding of Crimea is a process, and the Labour movement has still to be won to recognition that it is out of step in this respect with the Labour movements of the rest of Europe. Its leadership remains obsessed with outworn concepts, and continues to resist the flowing tide of history.'[23] One of these 'outworn concepts' was that 'progress' would only come from the Labour Party, and the CP much objected to this. 'While welcoming the progressive platform adopted by the Labour Party for the coming election', ran an official Communist statement, 'we regret that the Labour Party has not yet decided to take steps to establish the electoral unity of all organisations supporting such a platform.'[24].

With this policy the Communists set themselves against Labour's bid for victory, and at the same time against the highest point of working class radicalisation attained in the country in the last fifty years. It was clearly laid down in a statement put out by their executive, noteworthy both for its refusal to draw class lines and its insensitivity to the feelings of millions of soldiers and workers:

'The Communist Party, following a wide discussion among its members on the significance of the historic Crimea Conference, is of the opinion that national unity, essential for winning the war,

will be equally essential in the critical years following the General
Election to complete the victory and win the peace . . . At the
General Election it (i.e. the National Government) must be replaced by a Labour and Progressive majority, on the basis of
which we believe a New National Government should be
formed.

This new National Government should include representatives
of all parties supporting the decisions of the Crimea Conference,
international economic co-operation, and an agreed minimum
programme of economic and social progress for the people of
Britain . . .

'The Communist Party has proposed, and will continue to work
for, an electoral alliance of the Labour and Progressive movement, which it believes is essential to the winning of a Labour and
Progressive majority at the General Election as the basis of a new
National Government which will carry out such a programme.'[25]

All the stops were pulled out for a last assault on the independence
of the Labour movement, from their supporters in the constituency
parties, and from the positions they had gained in the trade unions by
their strike-breaking during the war. It was an opposition, in
Morrison's words, 'both fierce and unscrupulous'.[26]

But the ranks of the Labour movement responded magnificently,
and routed the coalition policy from the constituency parties, trades
councils, and trade unions alike. For the local Labour Parties had
been straining at the leash for some time, and a few had been
threatened with disaffiliation when they tried to break the wartime
electoral truce and put up against the Tories in by-elections. Frus-
trated by the attitude of the NEC, Labour militants had assisted both
the ILP and Common Wealth in their campaigns. Many branches of
the latter in particular consisted merely of Labour Party activists
meeting gleefully under a transparent label and pretending not to
know each other. Labour's decision to fight the next election was
greeted with jubilation. Talk of coalition was completely out of
touch. Harold Clay, chairman of the London Labour Party, was
speaking for the entire movement when he addressed its conference
on March 24th, 1945:

'We are not attracted by the suggestions which are being put
forward for what is termed a 'Government of National Unity'
whether they emanate from the leader of the Conservative Party
or from Mr. Pollitt, who is demanding a continuation of coalition
whatever the result of the election. On the broad issue of

international policy there may be a larger measure of agreement between the parties than at any other time, but on questions relating to economic and social policy at home the differences are profound . . .' ('Forward with Labour', in the TGWU *Record*, April, 1945, p. 191.)

While local Labour parties were practically unanimous against coalition, union after union resisted the Communist policy at their annual conferences.[27] A good example of the CP's attempts was in the Fire Brigades Union, which came under their control during this period and remained so until the fifties. A resolution put up by the South East and Scottish areas calling for Labour to 'assume an independent socialist role' was subjected to amendment by the Northern region and areas 1 and 2 to read 'accept union of all progressive parties', and a paragraph calling for Labour to break with the coalition government and 'launch a campaign for Socialism and Peace' was to be deleted altogether (Annual Conference agenda, 5th-7th October, 1944, no. 88, p. 20). Yet the only major unions to accept the Communist policy were the NUR and the AEU, and even here the position was only maintained by refusing to consult the wider membership on it at all.[28]

From the innumerable examples of the struggle at a local level we have space for only a couple here. The following, from a militant in the midlands can serve as typical:

'This was at the end of the war, with the election of a Labour Government . . . I moved from my branch a resolution to the Trades Council condemning the Communist Party for splitting the vote, in view of the fact that their policy was no different from the Labour Party's. In fact, it was quite the reverse, because at this stage they were calling for a government composed of "all progressives", which included Churchill and Anthony Eden, and so on. So I moved this resolution, and we got quite a lot of press coverage, because it was a resolution in a Stalinist stronghold, the Birmingham Trades Council, criticising them. The day I moved the resolution was the best-attended Trades Council meeting they ever had—it was absolutely packed. I got up and moved the resolution, and showed up the most disruptive activity of the Communist Party in Germany, when they united with the Nazis to bring down the Social Democratic Government, and their role in France and Spain—all that was brought out, and when the resolution was put to the vote there was a resounding victory— overwhelmingly carried, and I'm pleased to say that the Communist Party was never the same again in Birmingham. It was the beginning of the end for them, and in view of the fact that during all those years I had been persecuted by the swines, it was quite a joyous occasion.'[29]

The struggle was carried even into the ranks of the army. Another example comes from a soldier serving with Eighth Army in Italy:

'There were big debates taking place, and I remember one day speaking (on) . . . "What Do We Owe to the Germans?", and I used that as the title for my talk. . . . I said if Germany had given us only Marx and Engels we could never repay the debt. That was what we owed the Germans. The biggest chauvinists were the Stalinists. One man there, who was a member of the London District Committee of the Communist Party, attacked me bitterly. He said "What was behind this? Why do we have to have this sort of talk?". He was trying to imply that I was a German agent planted in the midst of British soldiers. Then afterwards, we had a debate, just before the General Election. Shindler and I put forward the case for a Labour Government, and this fellow was opposed and argued that what we need is a National Government—the Labour Party, the Communist Party, the Liberal Party and "Progressive Tories" like Churchill and Eden. He said that "You'll never have a Labour Government, the Labour Party by itself will not win against Churchill"—and he said this right up to the election'.[30]

Labour met in Conference to ratify its new election strategy in May 1945. Jack Tanner of the AEU led the fight to refer back the ruling of the Conference arrangements (the famous 3-year rule) and discuss again the question of "Progressive Unity". But the feeling of the delegates was all against it. Some, like Laski, it is true, did not want to bind the Party's hands, if a tied vote at the election made it necessary to come to some accommodation with other political forces afterwards. But this was a long way from the desires of the Communist Party, who wanted to fight the whole election on a coalition basis, and in any case Laski ruled out the possibility of any deal whatsoever with the Tories. The CP was far from being satisfied with this, and harking back to the old days of the Popular Front, described it as

'. . . an indication that the Labour Party Executive has in mind the possibility of a coalition with the Liberals and possibly other progressive groups. It is certainly a big step forward from the days of Chamberlain, when the Labour Party Executive rejected the idea of a People's Front on the ground that it would include the Liberals. But it makes the rejection of electoral unity even more ridiculous than ever. For if there can be a progressive coalition after the Election, why not electoral unity to ensure a progressive victory is won?'[31]

But the opinion of Conference was that a coalition would be a last resort if all else failed, not a goal to be aimed at as desirable from the first. As Morrison remarked in the debate, 'Only a coherent united working majority can give effect to that programme, and unlike the Communists we are not so reactionary as to seek an alliance with the Tories and Liberals merely because they accepted the Crimea Conference'.[32]

In the event Tanner's reference back was defeated by 1,314,000 votes to 1,219,000, and the Party went into the election in a spirit of optimism and confidence, willing to take on all comers with the enthusiastic support of the labour movement. A wave of class consciousness engulfed even the Executive, and found expression in the address of the Chairman, Ellen Wilkinson—an address traditionally devoted to ceremonial matters:

'In the coming Election the Labour Party will fight, and fight for power. We are not interested in talk of coalitions and arrangements, we fight for power: power for those who fought, and worked, and led, power for the workers in the widest sense, for those who work with hand or brain, for the inventors and the technicians, yes, and for the managers too who do not want to see the fine work they have done in planning for the public interest thrown back into the scramble for private profit'.[33]

But the Communist Party fought this feeling to the end, putting up its 21 candidates to split the vote to let in Tories and Liberals and doing its best to lessen Labour's chances by sowing despondency. 'Does the Labour Party then wish to rally all progressives?', asked Arthur Clegg. 'The Declaration says yes, but actually refuses to rally them. It suggests that "all progressives" should vote only for Labour candidates and no one else. It proposes not unity, but submission. This is armchair strategy of the blindest variety. It ignores both the realities of present day politics (the existence of energetic established parties prepared to work with the Labour Party) and the need to secure the widest enthusiasm if the Labour programme is to be translated into fact'.[34] The obtuseness of the Communist Party, in the face of an unprecedented upsurge of class support for Labour, led to another of those logical reversals that could hardly be described as dialectical. For whilst doing their best to split the working class vote for the benefit of Labour's antagonists, so that the Party would be forced into coalition by failure to gain the majority, they had the gall to blame the Labour Party for it! 'If Labour wants to defeat the Tories', wrote Emile Burns, 'it must repudiate the line put forward by Greenwood at the Conference of Labour women in London last weekend. He is reported to have said: "We shall fight all comers". This sounds very valiant, but it is the height of political stupidity to split the anti-Tory votes'.[35] They continued to press their policy throughout the election, to put pressure on local parties 'for democratic local selection conferences to determine the best candidate',[36] and to charge the Labour Party with being the splitters. 'It is a thousand pities', complained Pollitt, 'that we do not go into this battle a united Labour movement which has reached agreement with other progressive forces. This cannot but be an advantage to the Tories, who will be opposed in many cases by two or three candidates.'[37] Bathos was introduced by a party statement that described how

'In the constituencies where Labour and Communist candidates have opposed each other, all sincere members of the movement felt unhappy at a situation which has been forced on the movement by the stubborn attitude of the Labour Party Executive'.[38]

Right up to the eve of poll the Communists continued to sow doubts, line up with the Tories in blaming Labour for the end of the coalition, split the vote, and confuse the issue, attacking Labour's first bid for independence since 1935. A statement put out at the end of May summarised the Party's position:

'Their victory would have been certain and overwhelming if the Labour Party Executive and Conference had faced up to the question of electoral unity with the same realism that they showed on the issue of the date of the election. Unfortunately, the Labour Party Executive, by a majority, remained stiff-necked on this issue, and succeeded by a very narrow majority, in getting Conference to refuse discussion on it. This decision will cost the Labour Party more seats, not only on split votes, but because in the absence of a national agreement many progressive voters will not vote at all in constituencies where a candidate of their own party is not standing'.[39]

While the Communists were doubtful about Labour's chances, they were confident of their own. 'Those who are affected by this outlook', wrote Pollitt, 'fail to see the new and rising strength of the Labour movement and the thousands of new vigorous and capable men and women who are rising to leadership in the movement'.[40] Emile Burns' expectations ranged further. 'The splitters of the Labour Party Executive are likely to get a shock at the results',[41] he wrote. 'Some Communist gains are practically certain, and also many Labour victories. . . . it is common knowledge that the swing in the forces is very much towards Labour-Communist'. He revealed the extent of the party's ambitions by adding that Britain was the only country in Western Europe bar one that did not have Communists as yet in its government.[42]

In this way Labour faced its enemies, with the Communists working for them in its own ranks. A special cyclostyled broadsheet was put out during the election to add to the rest of the Party's anti-CP literature,[43] entitled *Communists in War*, reminding people of 'the eternal disgrace' of the CP's war record, their somersaulting, and the 'miserable crooked stuff' of their propaganda when they 'in effect played Hitler's game'.[44] Where it seemed likely that Pollitt himself would succeed, in the Rhondda, they sent down Laski to speak for the Labour candidate in person, and he went over the CP's war record to such effect that Pollitt was defeated by the narrow margin of 972 votes.[45]

Meanwhile, Labour was sweeping the country in scenes of wild enthusiasm. Reg Groves recalls how, canvassing his impossible constituency in Aylesbury again, soldiers came out of the gates of their camps, throwing their hats in the air to cheer him on his way.[46] Hatred ran so strong for the Tories and all their works that in Churchill's own constituency, where Labour had refused to put up a candidate, an unknown stood, paid his deposit, did no canvassing at all, and yet gained 10,488 votes. In the country some 12,000,000 voted for Labour, bringing it a parliamentary representation of 393 MPs. Apart from Gallacher, who stood for his old seat, the sole Communist gain was Phil Piratin, standing for an East End constituency with an exceptionally small electorate. It was the high point of the party's electoral fortunes. From then on there was only one way—down.

For it is at times of crisis, of the extreme polarisation of class forces, that the working class shifts its political allegiance from its traditional institutions. Then only can another party step into the shoes of the old; but only if it goes along with (and promotes) the unity of the class forces, and presents them with a viable left alternative. This was the time when Labour MPs, returned to the Commons in undreamed-of numbers, burst into the joyful singing of the 'Red Flag'; when had the Labour leaders so wished, they could have brought in the Socialist transformation of society with the minimum bloodshed and the loyal support of all outside the narrow coteries of title and profit. Even then, it was the major reforming government of modern times. But the Communist Party was on the other side in this conflict. It built up for itself thereby a legacy of suspicion within the Labour movement that has persisted to this day.

For the time being a bold face had to be put on things, and the party trudged on with diminished hopes in the future. An EC resolution hailing the result described how 'Labour's victory at the General Election, routing the Tory Party and giving Britain its first majority Labour Government, has been greeted with joy by democratic people all over the world'.[47] Rust's explanation was that 'the big swing to Labour caught up many voters who had tended to go Communist',[48] whilst Emile Burns carried off first prize with the remark that

'. . .let us remember with pride that it has been the work of the Communist Party through all those years that has gradually built up this understanding and this determination to 'End Tory Rule', the principal message in all our campaigns.'[49]

Not until the 28th August, a month after the election, did the Executive of the Communist Party give the signal to assess what went wrong, and admit to having made a mistake. The discussion period preceding its 18th Annual Congress released a flood of doubt from the rank and file, showing what tensions this impossible electoral policy had placed upon the ordinary member. A letter under the title of 'Following at the Tail', from G. D. N. Clark asked the party to 'witness the energy that was spent in persuading many sceptical branches of the need for a post-election National Coalition; where it was realised that this was incorrect, one had the odd sensation of being led to the Left by the Labour Party'.[50] Most revealing of all was a contribution from McIlhone, both in the extent of its criticisms and the realisation that something fundamental had gone wrong:

'. . .We held out no prospect of decisively defeating the whole Tory machine and bringing about the decisive Labour majority which was the expressed will of the labour movement. Instead, a prospect of Labour having to co-operate with the Churchill-Eden group of Tories after the war. This in effect meant that we were relying not on the forces of the working class, but on a combination of forces drawn from all classes and groups. Here we were not only out of step with the mood and sentiment of the working class and of the labour movement but, in effect, put ourselves into the position of opposition to these moods by the vigour of our defence of 'National Unity' after the war.

For us the big turning point, for a new valuation of the situation, and further development of our policies, was the Crimea Conference. For the working class and the labour movement the big turning point was the end of the war against Germany and the General Election which this brought.

For us the General Election was the opportunity to get rid of reactionary Toryism and create a new form of National Unity in which the 'progressive Tories' would co-operate. For the working class and the labour movement the General Election was the long-awaited opportunity to get rid of the entire Tory Machine. That is the essential difference between our conception and the policy and the moods of the working class.

For the development of our policy we tended to rely on a combination of groups and classes to begin the settlement of the post-war questions and less on the development of an independent working class line for this, with a slurring over, under-estimation, of the forces of the working class'[51]

Even Pollitt, in his Political Report to the Party Conference, had to admit that supporting 'a Coalition Government, including the Tories' was a 'political mistake', stemming from 'an 'under-estimation of the growth of political consciousness in the working class', an exaggeration of 'the degree of the differentiation in the Tory Party and the support for the Liberal Party', which 'did not take fully into account how quickly the reactionary forces could resume their old political struggle against the working class'.[52] But he made an empirical, sociological analysis: estimating the forces of such and such a class, the degree of support for such and such a party, the pace of differentiation within such and such a group. Nowhere was there a realisation that what was involved was treachery to the unity of the working class at the highest point of its political struggle. 'The mistakes we did make, he added, 'were infinitesimal compared with the great and lasting character of the contribution that the Communist Party made towards the winning of the war.'[53]

The events of 1945 set the pattern for the labour movement for the next generation. In the long run, if not immediately, the Labour Party spread out to take over what was virtually a monopoly of the political forces of the working class. By the fifties, Communists had lost both of their MPs, and by the seventies were left in control of only a few of the smaller craft unions. The ILP disintegrated in stages, the first to desert being the MPs and Brockway. The Party wound up its separate organisation in the seventies and joined the Labour Party as a publishing association. The Trotskyist Revolutionary Communist Party ended its existence in 1949, to be succeeded by a number of sects of more or less middle class composition and preoccupations. More unions came to seek affiliation to the Labour Party, even among the managerial and white collar strata, than had ever associated with it in the thirties. The 'tide of history' made so much of by the Communists had flowed against them.

They had prepared a case for their own rejection when they made their last great attempt to enter the Labour Party at the Conference of 1946. The National Executive was ready with the whole doleful record of their activity going back through the war and beyond. A month before conference met National Headquarters issued a pamphlet by Laski under the title of *The Secret Batallion*, which hung out their dirty linen for all to see. 'They have turned somersaults so vast in their intellectual agility', he wrote, 'that it has not seldom been difficult to know where they stood at any given moment.' He described how they had urged 'that the Labour Party and Mr. Churchill should form a coalition at the end of the election', despite 'the impossibility of reconciling the major principles of Mr. Churchill with those of the Labour Party.'[54] Finally, he made great play with the fact that not a single one of their major changes in policy had been debated before, or agreed upon, by their rank and file. 'It was not the mass of members in the Communist Party', he pointed out, 'who changed its policy from support for into hostility against British participation in the Second World War, between September and October 1939; nor was it the mass of members who removed Mr. Pollitt from the Leadership of the Party and compelled him to sign and publish a humiliating recantation of the views he had so emphatically expressed only a month before. These were actions taken by the Central Committee without any consultation with the rank and file. The only obligation of the rank and file was to obey without scrutiny orders thay had no part in making.'[55]

The debate on Communist affiliation at the June 1946 Labour Party Conference was a foregone conclusion, but even if it had not been the issue was made sure by Morrison's last great speech against the Communists. His words carried more than their usual weight, uttered as they were by the man who was responsible above all for the organisation of Labour's electoral victory. 'In connection with the preparations for the last General Election', he noted, 'when they were seeking to give us their support, they advocated a line of policy which was inconsistent with the principles either of Karl Marx, the doctrines of class-consciousness, or the doctrines of the class struggle.' He quoted at length from Pollitt's *Answers to Questions*, where he had advocated a National Government drawn from all parties supporting the Yalta Accords, and developed his point:

'Behind this policy for the General Election there was, there, first of all, a belief that Labour could not get a clear parliamentary majority. That was defeatism, just before the election began. Secondly, the policy was based on the belief that there should be another National Government, another coalition of Tories, Labour, Liberals, Independents and others—in fact, according to the parliamentary vote, the only people who were to be specifically excluded were the mild, small, unoffending members of the ILP, which I thought was rather rough on them.

This was the political mind of the people who were anxious to support the Labour Party at the last election.'

Then he went through a catalogue of the anti-working class behaviour of the Communist Parties abroad, the wartime zigzags, Springhall's espionage, and even the careerism of the CP's members in the unions. 'Among their slogans', he added, 'they ought to have "Join the Communist Party and do your best to get a job in the Trade Union Movement".' His conclusion was incontrovertible:

'The risk is that we of the Labour Party would be in a position of joint responsibility for their foolish and pernicious escapades with serious political disadvantages to the Party and very grave electoral embarrassment. The Party may not always easily dissassociate itself from the more serious actions of its affiliated organisations.'[56]

Jack Tanner's defence of the Communists on behalf of the AEU could only fall flat after this. The vote for affiliation was lost by the huge margin of 468,000 to 2,678,000.

But the final blow was a fundamental change in the organisational rules of the Labour Party taken in the aftermath of this debate. For it closed off for the future the possibility of any other political force being able to join the Labour alliance. By a similar vote, 2,413,000 to 667,000, the Party decided to allow no further affiliations from any other National Political Body after a date set at January 1st, 1949. It was the end of an epoch in Labour history. From then on, there was no possibility of a challenge being mounted to the domination of the Labour Party over the political consciousness of the working class—from outside its ranks, at least.

The Communist Party soldiered on, its numbers dwindling year by year. For some time it lacked even a political reason for existence, for it was in no way to the left of Labour. Though it had failed to make any impact on the electoral plane, R. W. Robson continued to preach that 'democracy is the watchword by which the common people will advance to the reconstruction of the world';[57] and even after the Atom Bomb had been dropped, it was years before the Party took a stand against the spread of atomic weapons:

> 'Scientists, who were slandered in many a monopolist's newspaper when the discovery of atomic energy was announced, are proving where they stand. They are campaigning in many countries against an Atom Bomb Monopoly, and want the knowledge given to all countries.'[58]

They did not even support industrial action for some time, hoping to gain some advancement by continuing to offer to the government and the employers the same services they had done in wartime. The first signs of disagreement between the unions and the new government suggested to Pollitt that 'the part played by CP members on the leadership of some of the most important unions will be a big factor in bringing these differences to an end',[59] and he kept up his opposition to strike action even on the floor of the Communist Party's annual congress:

> 'You are either in favour of the line of the report, or of the line that has been expounded here of mass strikes as the only way to realise the workers' demands. If the latter, I warn you, you are playing with fire that can help to lose the peace and reduce the country to ashes.
> Nothing is easier in the present situation than strikes, and our comrades should be most guarded. We should be ready to pay tribute to comrades like Scott and Horner and Hannington who in their difficult and responsible position are having to fight for the full utilisation of the machinery. You can get a strike in the coalfields tomorrow if you want it. Will it advance the working class movement of this country, or the perspective of our nation being a first rate nation in the family of United Nations?
> On the dock strike, I took the view that if our Party had been compelled to stick its head out in difficult situations in the War and compel our comrades to be stigmatised as strike breakers, we are not compelled to repeat that in days of peace, but we would examine every dispute on its merits. The *Daily Worker* reported the facts. It is true we gave no lead for ten days, but that is no crime, because we considered that strike ill-advised. If some of

our comrades were in difficulties on the docksides, well, Communists are always in difficulties, and we have to be prepared to face them and stand up against them.'[60]

The rest of the congress was behind Pollitt when it agreed that 'National Unity' was just as necessary in peace as in war.[61]

While its line remained no way to the left of Labour, the Party was redundant. It only came round to supporting strikes again when Stalin fell out with his old wartime allies, and the Cold War began. Even then, its hostility towards American Imperialism was couched in terms of British chauvinism—the defence of British national independence, interests and values, against engulfment by the American tide. It has lingered on with diminishing relevance to our own days, a political fossil, a failed reformist sect confronting a successful reformist party. The year of writing may have some significance here, for it is the first for a generation that no Communist has sat on the National Executive of the Engineering Union. If that is a watershed in itself, remains to be seen. What also awaits the answer of time is how long it will remain a monument to political inertia, until it experiences the fate of all whose over-specialisation prevents them from coming to terms with the process of evolution.

Footnotes to Chapter Eight

1 *Evening Standard*, 15th September, 1944.
2 *L'Humanité*, 19th September, 1945.
3 Frank Allaun, 'Why I am Leaving the Communist Party', in *Socialist Correspondence*, December, 1944, p. 5.
4 Herbert Morrison, Speech to the 45th Annual Conference of the Labour Party, Bournemouth, June, 1946—official report, p. 171.
5 As quoted in D. N. Pritt, *From Right to Left*, London, 1965, p. 297.
6 H. Pollitt, *Answers to Questions*, CPGB pamphlet, May, 1945, p. 45.
7 *Op. cit.*, no. 6, p. 48.
8 H. Pollitt, *How to Win the Peace*, CPGB pamphlet, September, 1944, p. 86.
9 H. Pollitt, *Answers to Questions*, p. 7.
10 *Op. cit.*, p. 11.
11 Frank Allaun, 'Why I am Leaving the Communist Party', in *Socialist Correspondence*, December, 1944, p. 6.
12 H. Pollitt, *How to Win the Peace*, p. 8.
13 *Op. cit.*
14 Above, p. 8, and below, p. 134.
15 H. Pollitt, *How to Win the Peace*, p. 75.
16 Report of the 43rd Conference of the Labour Party, Westminster, December, 1944, p. 37.

17 *Op. cit.*, p. 117.
18 H. Pollitt, *Answers to Questions*, p. 47.
19 Central Education Department of the CPGB, *Britain for the People*, 17th August, 1944.
20 H. Pollitt, *Answers to Questions*, p. 41.
21 *Op. cit.*, p. 41.
22 *Op. cit.*, p. 47.
23 P. Kerrigan, 'Crimea and Communist Perspectives', in *World News and Views*, vol. xxv, no. 12, 24th March, 1945, p. 90.
24 'Labour and Progressive Unity', in *World News and Views*, vol. xxv, no. 4, 27th January, 1945, p. 27.
25 *National Unity*, statement of the EC of the CPGB in *World News and Views*, vol. xxv, no. 12, 24th March, 1945, p. 89.
26 H. Morrison, Speech to the 45th Annual Conference of the Labour Party, Bournemouth, June, 1946—official report, p. 170.
27 *Op. cit.*, p. 172.
28 *Cf.* the exchange between Jack Tanner and Herbert Morrison at the 45th Annual Conference of the Labour Party, June, 1946, official report, p. 172.
29 Percy Downey, interview with Sam Bornstein, 26th November, 1977.
30 Charles Van Gelderen, interview with Al Richardson, 4th October, 1979.
31 Emile Burns, 'Electoral Notes', in *World News and Views*, vol. 21, 2nd June, 1945, p. 163.
32 H. Morrison, Speech introducing 'Let us Face the Future', statement of the NEC, at the 44th Annual Conference of the Labour Party, Blackpool, May, 1945—official report, p. 92.
33 *Op. cit.*, p. 80.
34 Arthur Clegg, 'The One Thing Necessary', in *World News and Views*, vol. xxv, no. 17, 28th April, 1945, p. 129.
35 Emile Burns, 'Electoral Notes, in *World News and Views*, vol. xxv, no. 18, 5th May, 1945.
36 H. Pollitt, 'Into Battle—With Confidence', in *World News and Views*, vol. xxv, no. 21, 2nd June, 1945, p. 161.
37 *Ibid.*
38 'Next Steps', in *World News and Views*, vol. xxv, no. 26, 7th July, 1945, p. 200.
39 'General Election', in *World News and Views*, vol. xxv, no. 20, 26th May, 1945, p. 153.
40 H. Pollitt, *Answers to Questions*, CPGB pamphlet, May, 1945, p. 47.
41 Emile Burns, 'Editorial Notes', in *World News and Views*, vol. xxv, no. 24, June 23rd, 1945, p. 189.
42 Emile Burns, 'Editorial Notes', in *World News and Views*, vol. xxv, no. 27, 14th July, 1945, p. 213.
43 Eg. Laski, *Stalin's Men—About Turn!*; *Is This an Imperialist War?* and *The Labour Party and the Communist Party*, and *The Communist Party and the War—A Record of Hypocrisy and Treachery to the Workers of Europe.*
44 The Labour Party, *Communists in War: How the Communists Played Hitler's Game When Britain was in Peril*, June, 1945, p. 2.
45 Laski spoke at Ferndale; only oral reports have come down through the movement about what he said.
46 Reg Groves, interview with Al Richardson, 2nd April, 1978.
47 'The Labour Government', Resolution of the EC of the Communist Party, 29th July, 1945, in *World News and Views*, vol. xxv, no. 30, 4th August, 1945, p. 233.
48 W. Rust, 'The Communists and the Election', in the *Daily Worker*, 3rd August, 1945.

49 Emile Burns, 'Editorial Notes', in *World News and Views*, vol. xxv, no. 42, 27th October, 1945, p. 335.

50 G. D. N. Clark, 'Following the Tail', in *World News and Views*, vol. xxv, no. 30, 4th August, 1945, p. 237.

51 'A Contribution from Comrade Bob M. Ilhone', in *World News and Views*, vol, xxv, no. 42, 27th October, 1945, p. 342.

52 H. Pollitt, Political Report, in *Communist Policy for Britain*, Report of the 18th Congress of the Communist Party, 24th November, 1945, p. 7.

53 *Op. cit.*, p. 8.

54 H. Laski, *The Secret Batallion*, Labour Party pamphlet, April, 1946, p. 14.

55 *Op. cit.*, p. 26.

56 H. Morrison, Speech to the 45th Annual Conference of the Labour Party, Bournemouth, June 1946, official report, pp. 170-1.

57 R. W. Robson, 'Democracy', in *World News and Views*, vol. xxv, no. 25, 30th June, 1945, p. 193.

58 'W. W.' (presumably William H. Wainwright), in *World News and Views*, vol, xxv, no. 43, 3rd November, 1945, p. 338.

59 H. Pollitt, 'The Road to Socialism', in the *Daily Worker*, 4th August, 1945.

60 H. Pollitt, 'Reply to Discussion', in *Communist Policy for Britain*, Report of the 18th Congress of the Communist Party, 24th November, 1945, p. 34.

61 Executive Report, *op. cit.*, p. 22.